Jey

Commerce
Law

to ninety —

$A_{1+2} + T$

1st ed. v.g. O.p-
sensational but
accurate.

614
54438 26 370
3K-2

$25 —

LIFE INSURANCE:
A Legalized Racket

By

MORT GILBERT

E. ALBERT GILBERT

Foreword by

ABRAHAM EPSTEIN

Executive Secretary
American Association for Social Security

MARLOWE PUBLISHING CO.

SCHAFF BUILDING

PHILADELPHIA, PA.

Printed in U. S. A.

CONTENTS

i

INTRODUCTION

The business of life insurance stands for more than a great American industry. Unlike most other industries, it is vested with prodigious public interest. In it are coalesced the hopes of millions of future dependents to whom it serves as a protector as well as the welfare of millions of farmers and home-owners for whom our insurance institutions act as creditors. Since practically all insurance leaders believe that the passage of the Federal Social Security Act will make Americans even more insurance-conscious than they are now, our life insurance companies may be expected to assume an even more important public role in the future than at present.

Because insurance is based entirely on mathematical formulae, most persons believe themselves unable to fathom its intricacies. They depend entirely upon the advice of the insurance agent who has only one interest in the matter—to sell insurance. This anomaly is bringing misfortune to millions of policy-holders. Unemployment or curtailed income is forcing millions of people to give up the insurance protection which they bought with little reflection in the days of prosperity. There can be no bigger indictment against any industry than the indictment which our insurance companies have brought against themselves in the waste which present insurance sales entail. During the year 1934 alone, the insurance companies doing business in New York lapsed and surrendered approximately 2,000,000 ordinary policies valued at over $4,500,000,000. During the same year a total of over 10,000,000 industrial policies valued at over $2,500,000,000, were lapsed and surrendered. Millions of other policy-holders have been forced to borrow about $4,000,000,000 on their policies, reducing to this extent the amount of their protection.

There was always imperative need of a book such as the Gilberts have written. This need has been accentuated by the depression. Millions of policy-holders demand information as to what to do with their present policies. This book should prove invaluable to the harassed policy-holders. It should help to enlighten the public on the fundamentals and merits of insurance. The public should demand to know why a mortality table which has been outdated for more than half a century, during which period the expectancy of life has made remarkable progress, is not modernized. There is urgent need for an understanding of the fundamental issues involved in insurance protection and savings. Education is necessary on the merits of "ordinary" vs. "endownment" and "limited payment" policies. The public ought to know the difference between the two roles of the insurance company as a protector and as a banker. The abuse of "cash value" needs to be stated and the story is eloquently presented in this book. The American people must be shown how they can reduce their present insurance costs and retain the protection they sought for their loved ones. There is great wisdom in the advice offered by the authors that decreasing needs may compensate increasing costs. The public should be aware of what is meant by "dividends" and should know the difference between "mutual" and "non-participating" insurance companies. Never before has the general public had presented to it so clearly the advantages of "renewable term insurance" as in this book. The light shed by this book on all these

iv

questions represents a genuine contribution to the preservation of insurance protection.

The authors cannot be blamed if the book leans toward "twisting." The unsavory term is not of their making. They plead for replacement instead of lapses or surrender. They seek to increase insurance protection by the retention of present protective values rather than by mere increased sales which lapse soon. The figures cited by the authors of new insurance written, lapses and borrowings cry aloud for replacement of the over-written insurance during the days when the flesh pots were fuller than they are today. Despite the writing of billions of dollars of new insurance in 1933, the total insurance in force for most companies at the end of 1933 was less than at the end of 1932. The Gilberts offer advice how to avoid the loss of insurance protection. Unlike the insurance companies which have created conditions bringing about such enormous losses through lapses and surrenders, the authors of this book seek to salvage existing insurance by showing how this can be done. It is the insurance companies not the policy-holders which have given this urgent demand for replacement the unpalatable name of "twisting." Let them make the most of it.

The authors of this book definitely treat this problem from a social point of view. They are seeking to meet a social need. While I find myself in agreement with the Gilberts in the advice they offer individual policy-holders, I cannot agree with their recommendations for social remedies. I cannot accept the conclusion that the Workers' Social Insurance Bill, sponsored by Senator Frazier and Representative Lundeen, offers the only adequate measure whereby industrial workers can secure protection. Nor can I accept their pessimistic conclusions on the futility of other legislative means. If the authors would look back one generation, they would find that remarkable progress in social legislation has been made despite all the difficulties. Witness the growth of workmen's compensation, mother's aid, old age pensions and child labor protective laws since the beginning of the century. Their advice to policy-holders to organize, it seems to me, will prove least fruitful of results. The American consumer does not seem to be organizable. Consumers' organizations in the United States have never been effective and the insurance consumer will prove even more impotent because there is great truth in the old dictum that insurance is sold and never bought. I believe that the Armstrong investigations did produce some good. Changing times brought new evils. This implies eternal vigilance rather than denial of governmental possibilities. A constructive, compulsory social insurance program for wage-earners, coupled with a system of voluntary insurance whereby the government is enabled to sell insurance to the better paid groups, can bring about genuine improvements in the insurance field.

ABRAHAM EPSTEIN
Executive Secretary
American Association for
Social Security

PREFACE

The overwhelming majority of life insurance policies in existence are far more costly than they need be. Their costs could be drastically reduced without impairing the protection carried. For rarely is insurance purchased in an intelligent, businesslike manner. Most men buy insurance blindfold, content to take the ballyhoo of company and agent as gospel. The companies' undivided 22-billion-dollar asset is the monument to the gullibility of policy-holders.

Life insurance investigators have long been aware that there is something basically wrong with insurance. They agree that it could be sold far more cheaply than it is. In their efforts to determine the reasons for its costliness, they have dwelt upon such superficial aspects as the extravagant costs of writing insurance, the excessively high salaries and bonuses of company officials, the domination of the large companies by the House of Morgan and the iron-fisted control of the small companies by the large ones through interlocking directorates, poor judgment in the investment of policy-holders' funds, the creation of remunerative jobs for relatives, and similar abuses of the insurance companies.

These well-meaning reformers and probers have done more to confuse than to clarify. They have inveighed against the stench—and have failed to see the dunghill. None has even approached the fundamental cause that makes the malpractices of the companies possible, that has virtually exempted our insurance companies from the world business crisis.

Previous investigators have examined the shady dealings of the companies themselves with the minutest detail. But they have never tried to analyze an insurance policy. They have ignored the source. It is within the confines of the 110 million policies that the fountainhead of most life-insurance ills is concealed.

The authors believe that this is the first book that examines insurance solely from the point of view of the policy-holder. Most of the sixty-five million men and women who carry policies are not getting their money's worth. This book is an attempt to discover why. It is a detailed exposition of the workings of life insurance, an analysis of the more popular kinds of policies, and a documented exposé of America's most respectable confidence game.

But it is more than that. It is a practical handbook for policy-holders—a guide to action. It tells you what is wrong with your present insurance—and it tells you what you can do about it under existing conditions.

You can cancel your policy loans without repaying them; you can retrieve all the cash in your policies without paying interest; you can maintain your present protection and reduce your premiums from 30 to 70%. This book explains how.

Mr. L. Seth Schnitman, in his admirable work, *How Safe Is Life Insurance?*, has aptly expressed the feelings of the authors:

> "It is not with the purposes of life insurance that we quarrel. Nor is it with the principles of diversified risks that we find fault. It is rather that the times demand a critical examination of the excrescenses that are rapidly enveloping the body life insurance."

The authors are grateful to the editors of *The Nation, The New Masses,* and the *Life Insurance Enlightener,* for permission to reprint the sections of this book which originally appeared in their publications. We also take this opportunity of thanking Mr. Abraham Epstein, of The American Association for Social Security, and Mr. Oliver de Werthern, Editor of *Life Insurance Enlightener,* who read the manuscript and made several helpful suggestions.

M. G.
E. A. G.

CHAPTER ONE

HOW THE COMPANIES BETRAY THEIR POLICY-HOLDERS

In the past, full of optimism and ignorance, you spent a frightful amount of money to buy "saving-and-investment" insurance. Even in the golden era of prosperity, you tried to put a little something away to prepare for a rainy day. The last six years have witnessed a cloudburst. The American policy-holder has been forced to borrow on his policies to the tune of $4,000,000,000. Having decreased his insurance-protection by that amount, paying an annual interest toll of a quarter-of-a-billion, the bewildered and overburdened policy-holder is looking for a way out.

What are the insurance companies doing to help the policy-holder in his hour of need? They are spending countless thousands of dollars (of his money) for radio broadcasts, full-page advertisements in magazines and newspapers. They are mailing millions of illustrated pamphlets, showing a widow holding her hungry child by the hand.

By way of a solution to the policy-holders problem, *they tell him to pay back the loan!*

Your policies are borrowed-on to the limit, your income has suffered a drastic reduction, you can scarcely afford to pay the premium, let alone the interest. You are frantically trying not to drop your protection—and their sole suggestion is that you return the loan. What a glorious end to a saving-and-investment program!

You sense that something is wrong, you have a vague feeling of having been trapped. You are badly in need of impartial, expert advice. Your accountant, with intimate knowledge of your financial problems, has ignored the liabilities and enormous waste in your insurance program. Your attorney, in many cases a life-long friend and confidant, is probably in the same boat, and hence can offer you nothing but sympathy.

Yet thousands of policy-holders, caught in the same trap, have escaped. What did they do?

TWISTING

Let us turn to Best's Life Rating Chart which gives the financial statements of all life insurance companies. We compile a chart concerning the ten leading companies (1933 and 1934 Editions).

	Insurance in force end of 1932	New Insurance Written 1933	Insurance in Force end of 1933
Metropolitan (N. Y.)	$18,980,743,208	$3,174,994,475	$18,802,984,818
Prudential (N. J.)	15,305,052,990	2,339,475,138	15,029,950,800

New York Life......	7,341,993,220	396,231,214	6,869,268,269
Equitable (N. Y.)...	6,665,098,062	591,369,612	6,196,495,744
Travelers (Conn.)...	4,369,338,963	457,533,518	4,148,918,298
Mutual Life (N. Y.).	4,226,616,174	168,312,553	3,903,658,087
Northwestern Mutual (Wisc.)	3,998,518,061	207,483,323	3,813,844,834
John Hancock (Mass.)	3,456,578,156	684,538,423	3,411,708,382
Mutual Benefit (N. J.)	2,334,602,527	191,894,308	2,165,831,398
Penn Mutual (Penna.)	2,008,947,312	140,916,321	1,897,343,490

What do these figures mean? They mean that in the face of a huge amount of "new business" written during the year, there is an actual decrease of insurance in force. Policy-holders are not adding more insurance to their overtaxed incomes: they are trying to avoid the high cost of their old policies by dropping their old policies. Much of the "new business" is "rewritten, retrieved and conserved" insurance, not new insurance.

When a company saddles you with expensive insurance, its most vital concern is that you keep it, and continue paying for it. The companies are greatly perturbed by the fact that thousands of policy-holders have successfully cut their insurance costs, and that many thousands more contemplate doing so. The method followed in most cases, the only practical method, is to rewrite—to buy new protection at a lower cost-per-$1,000, and to cancel the old expensive insurance. This rewriting is known in insurance circles as "twisting."

Against twisting, against every effort of policy-holders to lighten their insurance burden, the companies are waging a most determined and ruthless campaign. They have declared war against their policy-holders. We want to recount their tactics, to list the ways and means of their offensive.

* * *

By 1929 the high-pressure salesmanship of company and agent had so oversold the public that with the first crack-up of prosperity, the whole dizzy structure almost collapsed. Millions of people discovered they were paying more for their insurance than they could afford. The very fact that commission-mad agents had sold them viciously high-priced insurance had created an opportunity for a few intelligent agents. The crash made the opportunity golden.

These agents, alive to the situation, had found that they could make a living from rewriting, or twisting. What they did was to advise them to take out a new and much cheaper policy, and drop an old expensive policy. In most cases the policy-holder recovered his large cash value, cancelled his loans, and received new protection at a far less cost per thousand. Unlike the companies, the "twister" offered the worried policy-holder a practical way out.

What effect did this tremendous rewriting have on the companies? As thousands of policy-holders dropped old policies, they automatically cancelled their loans or retrieved their cash. In either case, the companies no longer enjoyed the interest earnings. And to add to their chagrin, much of the rewritten business was in lower-premium policies.

Despite the fact that thousands of policy-holders badly in need of help were getting it, the companies began a war on "twisting and rewriting." Criminally indifferent to the needs of their policy-holders, they determined to prevent the movement to retrieve cash and decrease costs.

The first shots were fired long ago when the companies began to flood the mailboxes of their policy-holders with misleading propaganda. The following stereotyped statement appeared wherever the policy-holder would be likely to look:

"Important—Notice

"This policy cannot be replaced by a policy in another company without loss to you. Beware, therefore, of any agent who suggests that you discontinue this policy: such an agent is not looking after your interest. He is thinking only of a commission he will receive on the policy he sells you."

Nearly all policy-envelopes bear that notice. If it fails to convince you, the companies mail along with your premium notice a circular entitled "A Policy Twister's Gain Will Be Your Loss." Deceptive literature of this sort has undoubtedly prejudiced many a policy-holder against seeking, or accepting, aid.

Anti-twisting propaganda, however, by virtue of its supreme disregard for the truth, has the annoying trick of coming back to plague the companies. The most publicized repercussion is the so-called Coolidge Incident.   In a radio speech delivered on October 6, 1931, by the late Calvin Coolidge, at that time a director of the New York Life Insurance Company, Mr. Coolidge levelled an unequivocal imperative at policy-holders:

> "Do not let anyone persuade you to alter or switch your policies without the best advice of the companies that issued them. Beware of the so-called 'twister' and abstractor or agent who offers to save money for you by replacing your policy in another company."

Shortly thereafter, Mr. Coolidge and the New York Life regretted the whole idea; Mr. Louis B. Tebbets, a St. Louis insurance expert, seeking "compensatory and punitive damage," had brought suit for $100,000 against them both. The case, like most cases involving insurance companies, was "settled out of court." Mr. Coolidge's letter of apology and payment of damages ended the suit. Mere policy-holders, fortunately for the companies, rarely seek compensatory damages for the harm done them by company propaganda; apparently, they are sufficiently propagandized.

But, of course, the chief fomenter of twists is the agent. Into the ears of their agents, the companies began to drum the following holy commandments (quoted from a rate book of the Equitable Life Assurance Society) :

"Points for the Agents

"Never speak disparagingly of any policy issued by any responsible company.

"Never advise a man to give up one policy in the Equitable to take another in the Equitable unless the change will replace a Term policy with permanent insurance. [sic]

"Agents who 'twist' policies should be driven out of business by their fellows. [i.e. If the change aids the insured at the expense of the company.] "Never advise a man to give up a policy issued by another good company to take one in your company.

"Never sell a man a Term policy if it is possible to sell him a Permanent [sic] policy."

Beyond question, thousands of agents incapable of seeing through the hypocrisy manifest in the above "points," swallowed hook, line and sinker. If you ask the average agent about twisting, he will reply without hesitation that it is impossible.

In the following requirement lurks another restriction to curb the policy-holder: "Full medical examination at the expense of the insured is required in case of change to lower-premium contracts. Change to higher-premium contracts as of original date may be made without examination." No more eloquent evidence could be summoned to show where the interests of the policy-holder lie. The companies stop at nothing to thwart your slightest effort to eliminate overcharges within your insurance, but offer every encouragement to get you to overpay more.

And yet in the face of this united-front of companies and agents to prevent you from getting help, "twisting" continued in ever greater volume. There were still a few agents who defied the commands of their companies and went ahead to help the policy-holder.

How did the companies deal with them? They finally resorted to the most despicable practice that can be employed by our vested interests. They influenced legislatures in many states to pass laws purportedly making it a criminal offense for an agent to advise you to change your policies.

Louis Brandeis, now Justice of the U. S. Supreme Court, in his book *Business—A Profession,* referred to this practice of the life insurance companies:

> "The quick assets, about $14,000,000,000 [now 22 billion] . . . is a menace because of the breaches of trust committed by men of high financial reputations, the payment of exhorbitant salaries and commissions, *the control of legislation,* and by the practice of *deliberate* and profound deception of the public."

The "anti-twisting" laws, thus passed, are never, and cannot be, enforced. In the few cases where "twisters" have been hailed into court on the ground of "misrepresentation" the company was forced to drop the case before the accused proved the company guilty of the identical charge.   Let us cite how one of the early cases ended (quoted from the Post Dispatch, St. Louis, Missouri) :

> "ANTI-TWISTING RULE UPSET IN INSURANCE SUIT. Special to Post Dispatch, Jefferson City, Missouri. . . . Circuit Judge, W. S. Stillwell of Cole County, has issued a 'permanent' mandamus directing the State Insurance Department to license Ray P. Prewitt of St. Louis, Mo., who was denied a license to write life insurance on the ground that he had violated a rule on 'twisting.'
>
> The insurance Department admitted that Mr. Prewitt spoke the truth in his dealing with policy-holders.   Judge Stillwell said: Violated a ruling?—It was nothing more than a frame-up on the public."

Is Judge Stillwell's opinion an isolated instance? Of course not.   The same thing is admitted (more or less) by honest actuaries everywhere.   The following statement of James E. Hoskins, Assistant Actuary of the Travelers Insurance Company, is typical:

> "There are men who feel that too strong objection should not be made to a substitution [i.e. a change of policies] when circumstances have changed or when it seems probable that the original insurance was not properly sold."
> —The Record, American Institute of Actuaries, Vol. 18, No. 38.

But by harping on these anti-twisting laws, the companies scared most of their agents into submission. It was now presumably unlawful for an agent to give honest advice. But the companies knew that the laws were, at best, an effective threat —when it came to a showdown in the courts, the laws were useless. A few courageously honest agents were not intimidated; they went right on twisting.

But the companies never run out of foul tactics. They said in effect, "Is the law ridiculous in court? Well, never mind the courts. We will pass our own private laws, we will be our own judge and jury." And so they struck at rewriting in the most effective way possible. The Metropolitan, for example, formulated a "No Credit—No Commission" ruling. This provides that after an agent sells a man insurance, if the insured, within six months surrenders any amount of insurance he had in force (in any company) prior to the purchase of the new insurance, the agent will receive no commissions for the equivalent of the amount dropped. (The Prudential outdoes the Metropolitan: their 1935 ruling specifies no time limit at all: ". . . if the issuance of the policy specified above replaces, or directly or indirectly causes the cancellation of a policy or policies previously issued by this or any other company, the company [The Prudential] reserves the right to adjust the payment of commissions as the circumstances of the case seem to warrant or to pay no commissions, as the company may decide.")

A more contemptible ruling has never been devised. Any agent who attempts to rewrite insurance is warned in advance that he will receive no commission on the new insurance: he will be paid not one cent for his work. The companies struck at the policy-holder by making it profitless for any agent to give him honest service. No man works for nothing. The companies made integrity such a costly thing that no agent could henceforth afford it.

As a matter of fact these rulings are even more vicious than they sound. They permit the companies to steal the commissions of agents who have no intention of rewriting insurance. Now, if an agent sells you insurance, necessity forces him to encourage you to keep your old insurance until he can get, beyond contestability, the commissions on the new policy. Therefore, the agent is not only prevented from giving you honest advice, he is prompted in self-defense to give you deliberately dishonest advice.

We want to cite an actual instance, showing how the "No Credit—No Commission" rule works in practice, and how it makes the agent the shackled slave of his company. In bringing this case to light, we do not want to jeopardize the position of the agent involved. Consequently, we have blanked out all clues in order to prevent the

Metropolitan Life Insurance Company from iden-
tifying him. This is, perhaps, a needless precau-
tion. We doubt that the Metropolitan would
dare to fire him, since it would prefer to avoid the
unfavorable publicity such an action would create.

As you read the letter take especial note of the
iron-handed fashion in which the company applies
the ruling. They admit that the agent had no
intention of a rewrite, and yet they dare confiscate
his commissions.

The reference to the insured concerns letters
which he wrote to the company, completely exon-
erating the agent of any suggestion of a replacement.

A photostatic copy of the letter is on the opposite page.

* * *

Now let us consider the case of an agent who,
despite the stratagems of his company, was still
determined to sell insurance from the point of
view of the client. The large amount of business
handled by this agent, indicates the tremendous
need for such agents. So many policy-holders need
honest assistance that any agent who can serve
them and get away with it, is overwhelmed with
enthusiastic clients. Such an agent had been doing
only what the company itself should have done
long ago—serve the policy-holder.

This agent wrote over half-a-million dollars of
insurance during 1932-33. For these years, the

METROPOLITAN LIFE INSURANCE COMPANY
FREDERICK H. ECKER, PRESIDENT

JOHN P. ROGERS
Assistant Secretary
MANAGER
HOME OFFICE
ORDINARY DEPARTMENT
In replying, please address.

Form O1234
May, 1933
PRINTED IN U.S.

NEW YORK CITY   August 10- 1934

IN RE:

Dear Sir:

Your letter of August 7, addressed to Mr.   Manager
of the Renewal Division, has been referred to us for attention.

We are really very sorry to learn that you have again written
Mr.   regarding the circumstances under which our business
was obtained, for this is the second letter you have sent us and
in which you ask Mr.   to write you.   You really should not
have bothered this man any more about it, because as we told you in
our letter of June 29, that even tho we were applying no credit, no
commission rule, and to which no exceptions are made, we did not in-
fer that your agent had acted unethical. You seem to stress the
point that your agent knew nothing of Mr.   intentions to discontinue insurance in other Companies, and we are not inferring that
he did, but the fact remains that insurance in other Companies did
lapse, and since it followed so shortly after the writing and issu-
ing of our business, no credit and no commission will be allowed.

Yours very truly,

John R Harris
MANAGER,
ORDINARY APPLICATION DIVISION

FB:EN

WHEN REPLYING TO THIS COMMUNICATION, BE SURE TO GIVE CORRECT POLICY NUMBER

officials of the Prudential Insurance Company
either were unaware of the circumstances under
which the business was written (or rewritten), or
were willing to ignore them, since it was business
twisted from other companies.   On the following
page is a touching letter of commendation written to the agent.

ORDINARY AGENCIES
GEORGE H. CHACE
ALBERT E. N. GRAY
ASSISTANT SECRETARIES
SAYRE MACLEOD, JR.
SUPERVISOR
THEODORE D. MILLER
ARTHUR L. STEPHANS
WALTER D. LEMON
ASSISTANT SUPERVISORS

THE PRUDENTIAL INSURANCE COMPANY
OF AMERICA
EDWARD D. DUFFIELD, PRESIDENT
HOME OFFICE, NEWARK, NEW JERSEY

February 20, 1933.

It affords me a great deal of pleasure to write you now
that the year has closed to congratulate you on having
reached a high place in yearly net issue amongst all our
Special Agents and Brokers.

The splendid work you have done is very much appreciated
by us all. I hope that we may continue to be favored in
the future with your business, and I can assure you that we at
the Home Office stand ready to aid and assist you in any way
we can.

With occasional glimpses of the sun through the dark clouds
overhead, we have high expectations for an improved 1933, and
we confidently look to you to continue amongst the leaders.

With kind regards,

Sincerely yours,

Sayre MacLeod Jr.
Supervisor.

In 1934 the agent's "splendid work" comes in
for more praise:

January 3, 1934

Dear Mr.—:
We are indeed pleased to congratulate you on
having qualified for the enclosed Gold Merit
Emblem showing $200,000, your net issue for
1933 having just passed that figure.
With it we extend the best of good wishes for
continuing success.

Yours very truly,

(signed)   George H. Chace,
Assistant Secretary.

But this could not go on. Observers believe that pressure from the other companies was exerted on the Prudential to drive this twister from the field. Consequently, it became extremely difficult for him to place business. So for a few months he made no attempt to write insurance, hoping that at the end of that time the pressure would be lifted.

When the agent made an attempt to resume work, however, he discovered he had been released. He wrote to the Home Office of the Prudential, asking why he was no longer in good standing. This was their answer:

August 21, 1934

Dear Mr.—:

Replying to your letter dated August 18, I wish to inform you that it is not our practice to continue to keep accounts open indefinitely without a reasonable amount of new business production.

According to our records, you have had no business issued to your credit for the current year.

Very truly yours,

(signed)   W. D. Lemon,
Assistant Supervisor.

The shabbiness of this pretext is obvious enough. There are agents in the service of the Prudential who have not written any business over a very much longer period.

The agent, depending upon insurance writing for his livelihood, again wrote, telling the company he had a large number of clients ready to sign applications. It seemed unlikely that the company would continue to use the "non-production" pretext in the face of a considerable amount of assured business. They did not: they didn't bother to use any pretext:

> October 3, 1934
>
> Dear Mr.—:
> Answering your letter dated September 28, we regret to inform you that we are not in position to avail ourselves of the opportunity of re-opening your account.
> Trusting, however, that you will be able to make other contacts,
>
> Very truly yours,
>   (signed)   W. D. Lemon,
>   Assistant Supervisor.

How impossible it is "to make other contacts" (with other insurance companies) is fully appreciated by those familiar with the interlocking character of the companies. So the agent was fired —possibly for "non-production."

The Company, in an obvious case of twisting, did not dare to admit its real reason. If it did, the case could be brought to court and truths unpleasant to the companies would be disclosed. For the officials of the companies know—and privately admit—the merits of the twist.

What happens when an individual is both a policy-holder and an official of a company? Whose interests will he serve first—the company's, or his own? The case of Arthur F. Hall, President of the Lincoln National Life Insurance Company of Indiana, is most enlightening.

In a signed letter dated December 1, 1933, Mr. Hall utilizes his position of trust to give the benefit of his experience to policy-holders:

> "Some of you will undoubtedly be solicited to drop your insurance. We feel confident, however, that your interests will best be conserved by continuing your policies in force . . ."

It is interesting to note the direction Mr. Hall's experience leads him to take when his own insurance estate is involved. He writes to W. J. Carmichael (February 27, 1930):

> "Yes, I personally surrendered $131,000 of insurance for its cash value of $24,000 and replaced it with $150,000 . . . I consider the $24,000 cash worth 5% to me, or $1,200 per annum. The premium on the $150,000 . . . is approximately $1,200 greater than the premium I was paying on the insurance surrendered. However, I have the $24,000 on hand plus $19,000 additional insurance, so I consider that I have increased the value of my estate over $40,000 by the exchange . . . it is true that an insurable risk has the right to take or drop such insurance as he pleases."

CHAPTER TWO

THE WAR AGAINST POLICY-HOLDERS

The life-insurance companies have launched a new offensive against policy-holders. This spring they pushed through the New York State Legislature a new amendment to the existing insurance law. According to Albert Hirst, counsel for the New York State Association of Life Underwriters, "the law aims to prevent twisting [rewriting of policies] . . . The amendment became necessary because of the rather startling experience that the New York City Association had in the prosecution of a certain Mr. Legg."

The Legg case, unique in many important respects, demands the attention of policy-holders. Mr. Legg, an independent insurance counselor, had advised a policy-holder to buy new insurance policies and cancel his old. The amount of insurance involved was $50,000. Without impairing this protection, the insured, by rewriting, reduced his costs by $728 and retrieved $10,870 in cash. The Mutual Life Insurance Company, from which the business was "twisted," took action against Mr. Legg. He was indicted for alleged violation of the state "anti-twisting" law, enacted in 1892, amended in 1923, and never enforced. The companies had never utilized the law in order to curb twisting because, contrary to popular conception, it is not an "anti-twisting" law at all. It merely declares it a misdemeanor to ". . . make any misleading representation or incomplete comparison of policies for the purpose of inducing [a policy-holder] to lapse or surrender his insurance."

By invariably referring to this law—and to similar laws in other states—as an "anti-twisting" law the companies have prejudiced policy-holders and intimidated agents. Thanks to the flood of company propaganda against rewriting, both the insured public and the soliciting agent are convinced that the practice is illegal. Rarely do the companies attempt to use the law as anything more than a threat. In Pennsylvania, for example, where an "anti-twisting" law has been on the statute books since 1921, not a single case has been tried under it, the companies being afraid even to test the law. Undaunted, certain companies in New York State determined to misuse the law to prevent Mr. Legg or anyone else from giving policy-holders further aid.

In the case of The People vs. Legg et al. (1931-32), the court had to decide whether Mr. Legg, in suggesting a rewrite, had resorted to "misleading representation and incomplete comparison of policies." The decision was based, of course, upon the consequences of the rewrite. Did the policy-holder gain or lose by the transaction? The perennial contention of the companies is that the insured "almost always loses." In keeping with this contention, they insisted that the twister must have violated the law, since only by misrepresentation could a policy-holder be induced to rewrite. If, on the other hand, the advantages promised by Mr. Legg were genuine, there could have been no material misrepresentation. Moreover, if he had no need to misrepresent, the implications are of tremendous significance in that they impugn the fundamental honesty of life insurance. Can policy-holders advantageously substitute new policies for old? If they can, we must conclude that the latter are basically unsound, that the over-payments, presumably for savings, made by the insured are not returned by the company at his death. For the most important effect of a rewrite is that the policy-holder salvages his overpayments.

The case finally reached the New York State Supreme Court. We will follow it through. Mr. Legg's contentions are taken from a statement he had submitted to the policy-holder, explaining and summarizing the replacement of policies. The Mutual Life Insurance Company had secured this statement and relied upon it as sufficient evidence to convict. The alleged misrepresentations in the statement were pointed out by an expert analyst, Joseph B. Maclean, associate actuary of the Mutual Life; his indictment included eight separate counts. The majority opinion of the Supreme Court was written by Justice Alfred H. Townley.

Legg, referring in his statement to the cash-surrender value of the policy, amounting to $10,870, had said, "You receive none of the earnings from this equity." Maclean claimed misrepresentation in that ". . . the insured received all of the interest earnings from the equity of the policy . . . part of it in cash as a dividend, and part of it as an increase in the cash value." The court held that Legg's statement was not open to that construction. In the words of Justice Townley:

> The statement itself in estimating the net insurance premiums upon the existing policy allows a credit of $570 for dividends . . . The obvious intent of the representation was that, until the insured had taken the cash-surrender value of his policies, none of the income thereof would be available to him for any use outside of his insurance policies . . . Taken as intended this statement was true.

(It is curious to note that Mr. Maclean, in an article published in the Eastern Underwriter, October 7, 1927, had presaged the court's opinion: "Part of the cost [to the insured] where the policy has a cash-surrender value is represented by interest on that value . . . The company actually holds the amount of the cash value, and earns interest upon it which is not paid to the policyholder. The insured, therefore, pays over the interest on his cash value just as clearly as if he held the cash value himself, earned interest upon it, and paid the interest to the company.")

Legg further contended that "in case of death, this equity, $10,870, is a loss to your estate." The company, aware that the fundamental principles of life insurance were at stake, tried to establish misrepresentation: "The equity of a policy is not a loss [to the insured] in the event of death, since it forms a part of the amount of the insurance, and, in fact, was the whole basis of the level-premium life insurance under which both the Prudential [which issued the new policy] and the Mutual operate." The court was not taken in by actuarial sleight-of-hand; its interpretation is in effect a recommendation of twisting:

> This statement [Legg's] is literally true. In case of death the insured would only receive the face of the policy [$50,000], and would receive nothing more . . . By surrendering the existing policies and taking out new straight-life policies, the insured would have insurance for the same amount, and at death would receive the face of the policies and have $10,870 in addition thereto, which would not be true if the present policies remained in force.

The remaining six counts of the indictment are not distinguished by their appeal to reason. We will skip them. Lest we be suspected of stacking the cards against the companies, we quote the Supreme Court's summation of the entire case:

> These alleged misrepresentations taken as a whole reflect nothing but a hypercritical examination of these statements [Legg's] undertaken in the hope that in a multitude of trivial criticisms might be found enough substance to support the charge made against these defendants. They are wholly insufficient to support the charge of misrepresentation or to indicate any criminal intent on the part of the defendants . . . The statements relied on by the people [*vide* Mutual Life Insurance Company] to sustain this conviction [of Legg in the lower court] concerned minor details and incidents connected with the insurance contracts which did not affect or destroy the substantial merit of the suggestion made by the defendants to the insured with respect to his policies . . . The judgment should be reversed, the information dismissed, and the appellants [Legg et al.] discharged.

It is significant that the minority of the Supreme Court could dissent only by accepting Mr. Maclean's testimony *in toto* without the slightest investigation of its validity. Justice Francis Martin, who wrote the dissenting opinion, seemed to hold that Mr. Legg's manner of approach to his client was enough to convict him.   According to Justice Martin:

> The indirect method of approaching the subject indicated that they [Legg, his associate, Stapler, and the insurance agent, Anderson, who was acquitted in the lower court] were not frank in presenting the proposition, and that it was being carried out through fraud and deceit. The attempt of these defendants to avoid each other while carrying out the details of the transaction and their failure to disclose their connection or identity emphasize the fact that they knew they were attempting to carry out a scheme or transaction which was forbidden by the insurance law.

Rich in unconscious humor, Justice Martin's opinion fails to mention the inexorable fate of agents who twist openly.   Legg's "indirect method" was patently an effort to protect the agent from the wrath of his company.

Beyond doubt, the outcome of the Legg case was, as Mr. Hirst called it, a "rather startling experience" for the companies. This precedent materially weakened the effectiveness of the existing law as a threat; hence the need for the amendment.   Intended to reinforce the "anti-twisting" law, to make it more difficult for policy-holders to obtain help, the provisions of the amendment merit scrutiny.   First, the amendment forbids the issuance of any illustration which misrepresents the conditions of any policy or falsely estimates dividends. No one can quarrel with that. A true representation usually makes an overwhelming case in favor of a rewrite. Second, it prohibits misleading representations as to the standing of any insurance company or of the legal-reserve system. An unstable system based upon fundamentally unsound principles cannot be perpetuated by legal benediction. Third, the amendment debars incomplete comparisons, that is, comparisons which do not include net premiums and gross premiums, growth of the theoretical cash value, disability and all other benefits, for the duration of the contract according to the expectation of life; to be complete, the comparison must mention possible differences as to amount or period of premium payment, including differences in incontestability and suicide clauses. The transparent intent of the companies is to compel twisters to analyze policies from a specious, actuarial view-point in the hope that, due to limited knowledge, the policy-holder will be taken in. Furthermore, the twister is obliged to warn the insured that, under the terms of the new insurance, he must postpone committing suicide for two years and that if he cannot wait, a rewrite is inadvisable.

A revealing light on the foregoing provisions is cast by the one which stipulates that the policy-holder is not presumed to know the contents of his policies. The companies seem unaware that their request for this provision is tantamount to an auto-indictment. Had the agent who sold the original insurance given "complete representation," had he presented "complete comparisons" with other forms of insurance, the policy-holder could not be ignorant of the conditions in his existing contract. Moreover, the chances are that he would not have purchased it. The stigma of misrepresentation comes back to where it belongs.

The real significance of the Amendment lies in its intentions and implications. Despite the "substantial merit" of rewriting, the companies are intensifying their campaign against it. They are determined to compel policy-holders to keep existing policies in force. They are prepared to go to any lengths in their frantic efforts to stamp out twisting. The large amount of space devoted to it in the insurance journals, the ingenious devices and tactics employed to prevent or hamper it, the legislation intended to restrict it, the propaganda designed to make it unpopular—all testify to the importance of twisting from the standpoint of the insurance companies. It is necessary to ask why they are so concerned about the problem. What makes them so anxious to keep policy-holders from rewriting insurance?

The answers to these questions are matters of vital importance to you as an individual policy-holder. The answers are certain to elucidate most of your own life-insurance problems. You have already gained some indication of what twisting does; in the Legg case, for example, you saw that it enabled the insured to reduce his costs and retrieve a large amount of cash, at the same time keeping his protection in full. Every year, you spend a considerable sum of money for life insurance; you owe it to yourself—and to your dependents for whom you buy it—to determine whether twisting is of practical interest to you.

We first raised the question of twisting in an article published in *The Nation* for May 22nd, 1935. The article, of course, brought forth wailing and lamentation from insurance-company officials. It also impelled an outstanding authority upon the social aspect of life insurance, Mr. Abraham Epstein, Executive Secretary of the American Association for Social Security, to comment; we quote from Mr. Epstein's letter, which appeared in *The Nation* for June 19th:

> "The interesting group of letters . . . published in the June 12 issue of *The Nation* are characteristic of the insurance fraternity. Whenever a few of the many defects of the present life-insurance business are pointed out in print, the insurance brethren promptly bring down a shower of indignant protests, and by the use of sophistry, play on words, and hocus-pocus mathematical performances they attempt to convince themselves that there is really nothing wrong with the most perfect of all institutions.
>
> "The Gilberts have raised one of the most im-

portant problems now confronting the life-insurance business. Everyone knows that life insurance was tremendously overwritten in the prosperity days. The total amount of insurance written rose from less than fourteen billion dollars in 1909 to over ninety billion at the end of 1931. That this insurance was written on a high-pressure basis, and that the huge sums written were never commensurate with the true ability to pay, is evident from the tremendous lapse ratio which existed even in the good days . . . As early in the depression as 1931, the number of ordinary policies terminated reached a record-breaking figure of 2,782,533, of which only 286,220, or 10.3 percent, were terminated normally. In 1933, according to the New York Insurance Department, a total of 2,402,879 ordinary policies were surrendered or lapsed. The story of industrial insurance was, of course, much worse. These figures are startling. Millions of people simply cannot afford to carry the insurance they have been induced to buy. That many lapses could be avoided by a change to a cheaper policy and lower premium is obvious. There is a bitter need for twisting.

"President Linton of the Provident Mutual Life Insurance Company of Philadelphia does not deny in his letter that the companies seek to prevent 'twisting.' Insurance executives continue to use the worn-out abili that they must do so in order to protect themselves against their agents. This theory is always perfect. Whatever is good in private life insurance is due to the mighty and high-salaried executives. Whatever is bad is due to the grabbing agents. But if the insurance companies cannot trust their own agents to protect the interests of their companies, how do they expect the rest of us to have faith in their represenatives as protectors of the policy-holders' interests? May I call Mr. Linton's attention to the famous O'Farrel vs. Metropolitan Life Insurance Company decision, in which the court declared: 'An insurance company which employs an agent of so little moral sense . . . ought not to be heard to plead exemption.'

". . . To the impartial student it seems that the Gilberts have raised a pertinent issue crying for a remedy. Will our insurance executives continue to boast about their production records, or will they help salvage policies which the depression is forcing millions of people to lapse, thereby losing the protection they tried for years to secure. The issue is vital and no amount of sophistry and hocus-pocus juggling will down it until it is settled right."

The attitude of the companies, as reflected in the Legg incident, cannot fail to convince anyone that the issue will not be "settled right" by the companies. The policy-holder, if he desires aid, can turn to neither company nor agent. His insurance remains his problem; he must solve it himself. Fortunately, it is within his power to do so, to plan his insurance estate, to adjust it to his particular needs. He has the privilege of buying or dropping insurance to suit himself.

The average policy-holder, however, knows so little about life insurance that he is virtually unable to use the privilege. He has an unselfish

desire to take care of the dependents and respon-
sibilities which he would leave behind in the
event of a premature death; he has the same praise-
worthy desire to provide for himself against the
uncertainties of old age. But good intentions are
not enough. You, as that average policy-holder,
are not accomplishing your two-fold fight against
insecurity with your present life insurance.

It is our purpose here to explain why not, and
to point out satisfactory remedies. It will be necessary for us to explain how insurance works; nowhere in our explanation, however, will we
employ the technical jargon that makes most books
on life insurance unintelligible to the average
reader. We do not intend this book to be a text-
book for would-be actuaries. We will include just
enough of the basic mechanics of life insurance to
enable you to correct your improperly written insurance estate.

While we will treat these fundamental principles
with as much brevity as possible, we cannot em-
phasize their importance too strongly. We know
how thoroughly the companies have indoctrinated
the public with misinformation. You have been
gulled into believing exactly what the companies
want you to believe. Your ideas on insurance have
come from those who had an axe to grind; from
companies with exorbitant profits to uphold, from
agents with fat commissions to collect. The
chances are not 1 to 10,000 that you know the

facts about life insurance—the facts that you must know to buy it intelligently.

We will try to present everything that policy-holders need to know about their insurance. Some of it you may already know. But we cannot afford to depend upon that possibility. *Neither can you.* Every truth about life insurance you don't know, every error you accept, is costing you money every day. Every dollar you spend for the wrong sort of insurance now, will deprive your wife and children of many times that amount in lost protection, when you die. We will work at all times on the uncomplimentary assumption that you know absolutely nothing about insurance. What you "know" now, you may have to unlearn before you understand the subject.

Our course will be opposite to that followed by the companies and their agents, who, profiting by your innocence, have thrown insurance into a bottomless pit of intricacy. They have perhaps convinced you that insurance is far beyond the comprehension of the ordinary businessman. All of which is nonsense. A reasonably intelligent high-school boy can understand insurance, so simple are its fundamentals once they are honestly explained. But not until you know these fundamentals will you be competent to analyze the actual cost of your present insurance and compare that cost with what you should and could be paying for it under present conditions.

CHAPTER THREE

WHAT LIFE INSURANCE IS: ITS NECESSARY COSTS

You have a definite, ascertainable money-value to your family. If you were to die now, your family would be deprived of the annual support you contribute. Your premature death is a contingency which must be guarded against. Life insurance is a social device originally designed to protect your dependents against the loss of money they would sustain in the event of your premature —as opposed to normal—death.

Like any other form of insurance, it is a system of protection against the risk of individual loss, distributing the burden of losses over a large number of individuals. Many people agree to share the burdens suddenly falling upon a few. In this way, the individual risk is *certain* but very small.

No one knows exactly when he will die. Death is an uncertainty. Yet there are few businesses in which the elements of uncertainty and risk really enter so little as in the life-insurance busi-

[42]

ness today. This is possible through the development of the science of statistics. "It has been found that there is no such thing as chance, statistically speaking, when computing the probability of death at any given time among a large number of people in the different age groups." The number of people in a particular group who die during a year can be determined with uncanny accuracy. By consolidating a large number of risks, we make what is a grave uncertainty for one, a minor certainty for all.

"All life insurance premiums are based on a simple and obvious principle, that the value of a company's expected income from a group of contracts must equal the value of the expected outgo on the same contracts." (Quoted from a company rate-book.) Your premiums for any year should equal your share of the death claims and overhead expenses of the company, and no more.

Practically all insurance companies determine what this "share," or your rate, should be from the American Experience Table of Mortality. This table was compiled by Sheppard Homans in 1868, while he was actuary for the Mutual Life Insurance Company of New York.

Without a table such as this one, rate-making would be a gamble, and insurance a mysterious speculation. Why is it that the table has made of life insurance the least hazardous form of business enterprize? The Mortality Table records how many people of a particular age will die during the year. It is "the instrument by means of which are measured the probabilities of living and dying." Applied to a large number of people this numerical probability becomes a practical certainty.

Let us illustrate; at the age of 35, the American Experience Table of Mortality shows that 8.95 persons will die out of each 1,000. Suppose, then, that a company wants to insure 1,000 persons of that age for $1,000 each. All it must do is collect $8.95 from each individual, adding the necessary amount for overhead expenses. Having collected 1,000 such premiums, the company would have a fund of slightly over $8,950. This will be just the sum it will need to pay $1,000 on each of the hypothetical deaths occurring for that age and cover its overhead.

And once the company has collected your premium, you have assumed your full share of the company's risk. The company will not lose a nickel if you die the next day, though it must pay your beneficiary $1,000. For 999 other people, of age 35, have also been assessed. A fund has been created to take care of that year's death claims, overhead expenses, profits, etc. If you die at this age, your death can cause the company no loss. They have a mortuary fund on hand, built up of your premium and 999 others, to provide for your death and eight others.

Just in case the role of the Mortality Table is not quite clear, we will resort to a homely illustration. Suppose you telephone your wife that you are bringing company home for dinner. Without giving her further details, you hang up. Your wife, of course, is puzzled. She doesn't know whether to prepare for two extra people or ten. She doesn't know whether to buy a three pound steak or a ten pound cut.

Later, she locates you and you tell her that you intend to bring four people. Her problem is solved. She knows exactly what she will need and can make adequate preparation. It is not material to her as she purchases the food, who these four visitors will be. All she need know is that her dinner must serve a given number of people.

That is exactly how the Mortality Table solves the problem of the insurance companies. It tells them the exact number of deaths that will strike any age-group. The company knows how many deaths to expect—and hence knows the exact amount of money it will need to pay death claims. There is no gamble, or mystery about it. The Mortality Table tells how many will come to the dinner of death each year and, without knowing or caring who these unfortunates will be, the company can prepare for them.

The fact that you die now, means that you are one of the nine theoretical deaths expected, and for which a mortuary fund was created. If you do not die this year, the company is still indifferent. For, according to the American Experience Table of Mortality, there will be nine deaths regardless of whether that nine includes you. So forever rid yourself of the false notion that the company is gambling on your life, losing if you die early, winning if you live long. The whole purpose of insurance is to eliminate that gamble. For the group, or company, the probability of death is a certainty determined by statistics. That is to say, the company's role is simply that of trustee for the sums collected; it holds a fund for one purpose—the payment of death claims: as a trustee, it cannot lose.

At age 45, to go on with the Table, the expected mortality will be 11.16 among 1,000 people. The protection-cost *must* necessarily be $11.16. Again, at age 55, the probability of deaths per 1,000 being 18.57, the cost levied *must* be $18.57. And so it continues. With increasing age, the likelihood of death grows greater, necessitating a naturally larger levy of premium. It makes no difference when you buy your insurance; at age 55, the mortality cost of $18.57 must be paid. You pay it. Whether you bought your insurance 10 years ago, last year, or this very year, that is the basic cost for insurance at age 55. You cannot beat the Table by buying insurance early in life.

The favorite argument of agents to get prospects to buy insurance when they are still young is that if they wait a few years, insurance will cost more. So much is true. *But it will cost that much more in those later years even if they do buy it now.*

If you want to insure yourself against fire-loss on your automobile, you pay to be protected over a specified period. When that period is over, you get nothing back—nor should you, unless your car was destroyed by fire. What you paid went to indemnify the losses of those whose automobiles did burn. You understand in fire insurance that there is nothing to be gained (except protection) regardless of when you buy it. In life insurance, as Justice Brandeis wrote, ". . . you get no advantage by starting early, the same is true of fire insurance." This fundamental truth has been obscured because the probability of death increases as you advance in age, necessitating an ever larger premium.

And this increased cost cannot be avoided—no matter what type policy you carry, or when you bought it. Are you skeptical? Your agent might tell you that such a statement is absolutely false. He might inform you that at age 60, the premium for a non-participating Ordinary Life Policy taken out, say, at age 35, will still be $20.06, its original price. By this half-truth most policy-holders are misled. The premium will still be $20.06, but the real *cost* to you will be much higher. This will be fully demonstrated in later chapters. You cannot avoid the increased mortality-cost, *be-cause it is the first charge the company must de-duct from your payments to meet the death claims of each year.*

This basic cost of life insurance is expressed in the American Experience Table of Mortality: low at an early age, progressively higher as the years go by. Hence, as 2 parts of hydrogen + 1 part of oxygen = water, which no amount of legerdemain can alter, so the mortality-cost plus overhead equal the true cost for insurance.

To make it clearer. The probability of death as expressed by the American Experience Table for ages 35 to 45 inclusive, is indicated below in the middle column. The rates for a $1,000 One-Year Renewable Term contract for the same span of years are shown in the adjoining column. Compare them:

Age	Probability of death	Cost of one-year Renewable term policy
35	8.95	$8.82
36	9.09	8.96
37	9.23	9.10
38	9.41	9.27
39	9.59	9.45
40	9.79	9.65
41	10.01	9.96
42	10.25	10.31
43	10.52	10.67
44	10.83	11.19
45	11.16	11.60

It may amaze you to discover that at age 45

you can buy $1,000 worth of insurance for $11.60.
But an analysis of the columns above reveals something more amazing than just the low cost for
actual insurance-protection. Note that for age 35,
the probability of death, according to the American Experience Table, is 8.95. Yet the cost for
$1,000 worth of insurance is only $8.82! That is,
according to the Table, the company must pay
out $8.95 in death claims, pay the agent his 30%
commission, and meet its fixed overhead expenses
—all out of $8.82!

What can this mean? It means that the Table
is out of date and needs revision. It means that
8.95 no longer expresses the probability of death;
that the present probability is much smaller. This
is nothing new. Even Mr. Homans, who compiled
the Table, admitted one year after its completion
that it was "inadequate." Yet, in the main, the
companies still charge you rates based on this
antiquated table.

The "inadequacy" of the Table arises from two
sources. First, the Table was computed upon 100,-
000 people chosen at random, regardless of physical
fitness. When the companies, on the other hand,
deign to accept individuals as risks, they do so only
after the most rigid examinations. They insist
upon physical fitness, financial stability, and moral
perfection. Were the companies to accept all risks,
the Table might be acceptable. But, since they reject all but preferred risks,* a new Table should

---

*Sub-standard risks are accepted at increased rates.

be used, based upon the mortality of such risks. It was probably to this that Mr. Homans referred when he admitted that the Table was "inadequate."

Secondly, compiled in 1868, the Table has not been revised to conform with the remarkable advances made in medical science. The achievements of X-ray, surgery, preventive and corrective medicine, improved hospitals and clinics, in prolonging life, are summarily dismissed. So that even if the companies did accept all risks, the Table would still be unsatisfactory.

Its "inadequacy" is nowhere better demonstrated than in the companies' own published figures for actual as compared to "expected" deaths. Below is the ratio of actual to expected mortality for 1933 of some of our largest companies:

	Expected Mortality	Actual	Gain in favor of Company
Metropolitan	100%	51%	49%
Prudential	100%	64%	36%
Equitable Life.......... (New York)	100%	61%	39%
New York Life.........	100%	62%	38%
Travelers	100%	68%	32%
Mutual Life (New York)	100%	69%	31%
Northwestern Mutual....	100%	61%	39%
John Hancock..........	100%	66%	34%
Penn Mutual...........	100%	67%	33%
Mutual Benefit	100%	63%	37%

In other words, the companies base your rates on the *expected* mortality, and pay death claims for actual mortality. In 1933, where the Metropolitan collected premiums for 100 deaths, only 51 policy-holders actually died. That is, the Metropolitan policy-holders overpaid 49% for unused mortality costs alone. Whatever that differential is in any year, then by just so much are you overpaying for their cheapest insurance. Why is this difference not returned to the policy-holder in the form of lower insurance costs?

Life insurance, then, is a mutual device to eliminate the individual risk occasioned by death. The company's role should be one of intermediary, or trustee.

We have discovered that the basic cost of all life insurance is mortality plus overhead. This cost is expressed, even though inadequately, in the American Experience Table of Mortality. We have learned that it is inevitable that, as we advance in years, the cost of insurance does and must go up. *No device has as yet been conceived to eliminate higher mortality costs with advancing years.*

Life insurance is protection against the money-loss a man's family sustains when he dies. The insured himself can get nothing from life insurance. The only return from life insurance is the death claim paid to a beneficiary.

Just as in fire insurance, where you can get no indemnity unless you suffer a fire loss, so in life insurance there can be no return unless there is a death.

We have attempted to acquaint you with what life insurance is. It is equally important to tell you what it is not.

CHAPTER FOUR

WHAT LIFE INSURANCE IS NOT:
ITS EXCESS CHARGES

Many "saving-and-investment" plans are offered you by the insurance companies. In their show-cases lies a display of more than seventy kinds of policies. You can buy an Adjustment policy or a Family Income policy; a 10-Payment Life or a 15-Payment Life; a 20-Payment Life or an Endowment at Age Sixty-Five—and for those who cannot make a choice between a Limited Payment plan and an Endowment, there is a policy labelled "Twenty-Payment Endowment at Age Sixty-Five." You can purchase an Educator policy or an Emancipator policy; a Retirement Income Endowment—endowing at any age you choose; a Single Premium Retirement Income or a Cash Settlement at Age Eighty; an Ordinary Life or a Life Expectancy—in short, as the companies phrase it, "There is a policy to suit any insurance need."

Each of the above policies bears its own price tag. The price range per thousand for age 35, is from about $9 to about $350. But each policy, irrespective of label and price, *carries exactly $1,000 of protection*.

Select any label you like; pay $10 a year or $50 a year: when you die your beneficiary will receive $1,000. You, according to the companies, have one "insurance need," while your neighbor has a quite dissimilar "insurance need." You pay one price; he pays another price: and you have both bought the identical $1,000 of protection. What price "insurance needs"?

The truth is that everyone has the same *insurance* need—protection. The *amount* of protection desired varies with the individual; but the rate-per-$1,000 of this protection, for a given age, does not. We have seen that the rate is determined by mortality-cost plus overhead. The wide range of prices must be due to a third element, one that varies greatly enough to make one $1,000 policy cost nearly forty times as much as another.

The element that has the peculiar virtue of increasing your costs without increasing your protection is the companies' mystical lure of "Cash Value." It is this that lies in progressive degrees within the price range. Were it not for the difference in the size of the cash values created, it would be difficult to tell the various policies apart.

No prospective holder of a policy has been exempt from the alluring descriptions and ballyhoo launched by agent and company to promote a bigger cash value in his policy.

What are these cash values?—upon what do they depend? When we tear aside the mysterious veil enveloping them and concealing their true nature, we find nothing but *excess charges*.

The amount of money you pay the company, over and above the necessary cost for protection (mortality-cost plus overhead), creates the cash value. These voluntary overpayments accumulate from year to year *within* the policy. "Cash Value" is the catchword used to steer you into high-priced contracts. But it is to your voluntary overpayments that the companies refer when they speak of "cash value," "reserve," or "savings." Especially do they like to call them "savings."*

For "savings" is a very attractive lure; so attractive, in fact, that most men, offered the choice between a low-priced policy with small "savings" and a high-priced one with large "savings," will unhesitatingly make the overpayments to get the policy with large "savings." And it is savings—to the extent that it is your money, deposited with the company. But unlike savings held elsewhere, it is so shackled with objectionable qualifications and conditions that it is scarcely recognizable as such.

---

*The Philadelphia Life Insurance Company, in a pamphlet boosting the idea of "savings," is a typical spokesman: "In the saving period, known amounts of cash value are available to you. You have a backlog built up from your own deposits— useful to you in case of need as savings should be." This is merely one example, taken almost at random out of a possible thousand.

The four main shackles are as follows:

(1) You purchased your higher-premium form, presumably to save for a rainy day. It pours. Desperately in need of ready cash, you rush to the company with your policy to avail yourself of your savings. You are confronted with a six per-cent annual interest-charge. Has it ever occurred to you that the companies are demanding interest on what they have assured you is your savings? *What method of saving, other than within an insurance policy, penalizes you with an interest-charge when you wish to use your own savings?*

(2) You have made sacrifices during life to save money with the company. In the event of your death, you forfeit every cent of that savings. Your beneficiary receives only the face amount of your policy. Irrespective of the amount of excess payments you made to create "savings" in your policy, only the amount of protection you originally purchased is returned to your beneficiary at the time of your death. *In what savings institution, other than insurance companies, would the depositor have to forfeit his savings at death?*

(3) Suppose you have borrowed $1,000 of your savings and are, therefore, paying $60 annually for its use. This would seem penalty enough for using your own money. Not at all. Actually you are borrowing from your beneficiary: the face amount of the policy at once becomes $1,000 less.

The amount you can borrow is limited to the

extent of the cash value in your policy.   According to law, the company is not permitted to lend money to the policy-holder.   It can "lend" him only the amount of his cash value (his own cash). And since, if the loan is not repaid, it is deducted from the amount given to the beneficiary at the insured's death, the loan is unquestionably made from the beneficiary.   Remember that in the first place the company sold you a high-priced policy by stressing the element of "savings."   Their deception becomes manifest when you realize that your savings is more imaginary than real.

The more you borrow what you think is your savings, the more interest you pay the company, *AND the less your beneficiary receives.*

(4) You have decided, as above, that you need ready cash.   But the company, as we have seen, penalizes you and your beneficiary in so many ways if you make a loan that you naturally hesitate to borrow your savings.   The only thing you can do to get back your savings unencumbered, is to surrender, or cancel, your policy.   The company will "buy it back" from you—with your own money.   They refund your savings.   The cash value is immediately yours—but at what a sacrifice! Your dependents are no longer protected.   That is, the very purpose for which insurance was created is defeated by the companies' impractical attempt to couple it with savings.   That is why, as Justice Brandeis has said, "The mortality of

policies is ten times as great as the mortality of men carrying them." Nine policies out of every ten taken out are not carried to their intended completion. We let the reader determine what percentage of the people now paying for insurance are wasting their money: to calculate how many widows will receive not one cent in death claims. This deplorable condition must be laid at the doorsteps of the companies themselves. It would not exist if the companies were content to sell life insurance as protection. *By preaching "saving," they are, in effect, exhorting lapse and surrender.*

* * *

The disclosures above reveal the faultiness of combining savings with protection. Each is good, in itself—as long as you keep them separated. This is no new truth: we claim no credit for its discovery. Men of national reputation in the business and insurance world have pointed it out time and time again.

Here is what Mr. Charles E. Brooks, Consulting Actuary, and author of *Life Insurance for Professors,* said about it:

> "In any attempt to devise a system of life insurance—a most important step is to effect a separation of those purposes which can be obtained only through insurance from such purposes as investment and saving for old age."

Mr. R. R. Lounsbury, President of Bankers' National Life Insurance Company, admitted the truth of the "shackles" in an article published in the *National Underwriters Journal*. His exact words:

> "As for the man who is really up against it, who wants to keep his insurance protection and at the same time realize money on his policies, he should realize that in borrowing cash against his equity *he is going at his problem in the most expensive way. He is paying 6% on the loan and his protection is reduced by the amount of the loan*." (Italics ours.)

The testimony of Mr. W. F. Gephart, a former Dean of the School of Commerce and Finance of Washington University, could not be more explicit:

> "Life insurance is not an investing institution. It can never return to the buyer a profit. As a protection device it has been greatly retarded in its true development by having had attached to it many of the appendages of an investment."

Rabbi Stephen S. Wise, advocating pure insurance to the Association of Life Underwriters at Detroit, stated:

> "I like life insurance—straight. It ought not to be mixed or sugar-coated or bound up with anything else."

An admission of the truth of our contentions came from the late Darwin P. Kingsley when he was President of the New York Life Insurance Company. He said:

"As trustees of the reserve funds of individuals, we are concerned over the increase in loans. They impair the policies by just so much." (Four billion dollars in 1934.)

But perhaps the most shocking example of letting the cat out of the bag is afforded by the Travelers Insurance Company of Hartford, Connecticut. This Company, like all others, sells its high-premium policies by stressing cash values. It also sells low-premium contracts which will contain little or no cash value. Let us assume that you are about to buy one of the low-priced contracts. An agent from a rival company chances upon you and tries to sell you a costly policy, one that will build up ever-so-much more cash value than the Travelers contract. The agent representing the Travelers is not unarmed. He refers to his *Agents Service Book,* a confidential handbook not meant to be shown to the prospective policy-holder. This is what his Company instructs him to do:

> "The agent of the [competing] company will probably try to combat this argument by talking cash values. Do not let the buyer of insurance forget that *cash values are only theoretical* unless he closes out his contract, *that he can avail himself of them only by giving up his insurance.*" (Italics ours.)

Get it? First they try to sell you the idea of cash value. Then, if another company offers you a policy with more cash value, they stand on their head and assure you that cash value is meaningless anyway, is just "theoretical"!

When it comes to selling a policy, both agent and company will resort to any weapon they can, no matter how it may confound their own argument for some other policy. No trick is too contemptible, no device too unscrupulous—most agents and companies continually use them: they are simply part of the tool-kit. In this matter it might be well to quote Mr. Roger Babson, famous publisher of business news and advice, who counseled:

> "Buy life insurance as protection, the same as you would buy automobile insurance, but think twice before buying it as an investment. With the greatest respect for the insurance companies it could do no harm for such clients to obtain the advice of an impartial expert."

All these statements hammer home the cardinal truth—*under no present circumstances should insurance and savings be combined.*

WHEN ASSETS BECOME LIABILITIES

What really happens when you try to save or invest within your insurance policy? In other words, how do the cash values you constantly create actually affect your estate? In order to answer these questions, we must consider the role of the policy-reserve. We will see in a later

chapter that its main function is to take care of
rising mortality-costs in the later years. On that
point there is some agreement among insurance
men. But they differ in their conceptions of the
mechanics of the reserve.

One group holds that, when the insured dies,
the company pays the full amount of insurance
named in the policy, and the insured forfeits his
reserve to the surviving policy-holders. In this
manner, the mortuary fund will be sufficient at
all times to pay expected death claims.

Many actuaries, and most company officials, dis-
like to admit that savings are forfeited. Their
conventional explanation is that the policy-reserve
is the insured's savings-account and constitutes a
part of the death claim; hence, the actual amount
of *insurance* in the policy at any given time is not
the face amount, but the difference between the
face amount and the cash value.

We will let Mr. M. A. Linton, President of the
Provident Mutual Life Insurance Company of
Philadelphia, present this point-of-view, usually
referred to as the savings-bank theory or the self-
insurance theory:

> "A policy on the life or endowment plan is
> made up in essence of two elements: first, a sav-
> ings-fund element which builds up the reserve
> accumulation that forms the basis of the guar-
> anteed cash and loan values, and, second, a net
> protection element. The amount of the net

insurance protection in any year is the amount by which the face of the policy exceeds the accumulated value. Since the accumulated value increases year after year, the amount of the net protection decreases correspondingly. The important thing, however, is that the charge for the net insurance protection is computed on the basis of the *decreasing* amount and not on a *level* amount. This means that when death occurs under a $10,000 policy, where there is, say, a reserve of $4,000 in hand, the company pays the claim by using the $4,000 and then drawing the remaining $6,000 from the mortality fund for the year. The two together make up the $10,000 paid on the policy. The policy-holder, however, has not been charged for net protection on a level $10,000 basis but for a decreasing protection; and in the year for which the illustration is cited the charge was for $6,000."*

This explanation raises several interesting points. The policy-holder must understand what Mr. Linton means by "charged." For the insured, neither knowing nor caring what the company is doing with his premium, pays a large uniform amount every year with the mere understanding that his beneficiary will receive a specified face amount at his death. Mr. Linton reveals that in the earlier years most of the premium buys "savings." Only in the later years does most of it buy protection. As far as the policy-holder is concerned, however, he is always being charged the

---

* In a letter to *The Nation* for June 12, 1935.

full amount of premium. Upon his ability to pay this amount rests his ability to keep the policy in force. For, while a dollar spent for investment can buy only a dollar's worth, a dollar spent for insurance can, between the ages of 35 and 45, buy about a hundred dollars of protection. Thus, what the company is doing with his dollar is the insured's vital concern: at his death, intimates Mr. Linton, he will not forfeit savings—he will forfeit a portion of his insurance. Mr. Linton's concept, therefore, in no way conflicts with the reality of forfeiture. J. B. Maclean, referring to the two views one can hold as to the character of the reserve (whether it is forfeited or used to make up the death claim), writes: "It does not seem to be of any importance which of the ideas is adopted— both are theoretically correct."

Let us amplify a bit so that we may determine how the matter affects you and your estate. When you purchased your $10,000 policy, you were led to believe that you would get $10,000 of protection, year after year. Let us say that it is an Ordinary Life contract issued at age 35, with an annual premium of $200.60. Bear in mind that the cost for $10,000 of pure insurance-protection at the same age is only $88.20. Now, then, assume that 14 years have passed and your savings feature, your cash value, has amounted to $2,000. Death occurs. According to Mr. Linton, your beneficiary would in effect get two checks: first, the $2,000 in savings: and second, $8,000 representing protection.

Mathematically, it may be fair enough. But if you had purchased Renewable Term insurance, for approximately half of the cost for Ordinary Life, and had saved the other half on the outside in a separate saving-fund, what would be the picture of your estate? Your beneficiary would receive the death claim of $10,000 *plus* the full amount of the outside savings with accrued interest. Whether the sum saved on the outside would be exactly equal to $2,000 would depend upon the rate of interest earned. The point to remember is that the sum would be a considerable amount, making the total estate larger than $10,000. If you wish, then, you can say that the beneficiary gets the $10,000 death claim, and *forfeits* whatever the outside savings-fund would have amounted to. Mr. Linton's actuarial concept of self-insurance entails a loss of money to your estate. Hence, whether you regard your cash value as self-insurance or as savings-to-be-forfeited, your estate sustains a loss at your death. If your death does not come at this time, *the savings represents a potential loss, or a liability.*

Suppose death occurred later, when your cash value had reached $3,000. In effect, the company would now settle your death claim with two checks: first the $3,000 in savings; second, $7,000 representing protection. Remember that your agent told you that your policy would always contain a full $10,000 of *insurance*.   Had you saved in any other institution, your estate would still consist of the $10,000 death claim with the addition of your outside savings-fund.   As long as you keep a reserve-building policy, you always face a potential loss.

You now see in what sense your cash values can be called self-insurance.   You contribute them, and the company applies them, toward the face amount of the policy when it matures as a death claim.   The difference between the face amount of the policy and the total amount of the cash value, represents the true net insurance, or the actual risk to the company.   If you had kept your savings on the outside, buying protection alone, the savings would be an asset to your estate.   In your insurance policy, what you think are assets are liabilities in reality.

On the balance sheet of your estate, there should appear under "assets," the amount of insurance-protection you have purchased and the amount of money you are saving.   The offsetting liability, being the total premium paid each year, is made up of the costs for these two items.   But, as long as you keep your insurance in force, the asset, savings or cash value, is illusory, or as the Travelers admitted, "theoretical," while the genuineness of your liability will be emphasized every time you have to pay the premium (including the excess charge for savings). Are you then paying for something which may never benefit your estate? You are. Actually, in your attempt to save within your policy you have only created a liability for your estate.

Although the concept of self-insurance, as we have shown, is merely another way of looking at savings-to-be-forfeited, it is extremely useful at times in the current-cost analysis of policies. We will reintroduce it wherever it helps to simplify the analysis. But, whichever way you prefer to look at it, you are dealing with the same liability.

It is worth mentioning that the insurance world is by no means agreed upon which way the reserve should be regarded; in fact, the insurance companies are inclined to use both viewpoints, changing from one to the other according to the dictates of the situation. As Mr. E. T. Dooley, California actuary, points out in his *Facts and Fallacies of Life Insurance*,* buyers of insurance are urged to believe that protection is constant—which lends support to the forfeiture theory. But when a policy-holder raises the question of forfeiture, the company takes refuge behind the savings-bank theory. In some states, there have been attempts made by the taxing authorities to tax policy-reserves on the same basis as savings-accounts in banks; where that is attempted, "the insurance companies, with chameleonic inconsistency, will

---

* In manuscript form, as yet.

be found blatantly declaring that these reserves are not savings accounts at all." In most controversies, Dooley continues, "The companies prefer the savings-bank theory, for a policy that entails possible forfeiture is not likely to appeal to prudent men."

Once you understand that your cash value is a liability as long as it remains within the policy, you have gone far toward a comprehension of your insurance problem. We do not believe that this point can be stressed too often. In order to clarify the several issues that have been raised thus far in the present chapter, we will quote a section from an editorial which appeared in the *Life Insurance Enlightener* for August, 1935. The editorial in question is a most excellent statement of the problem from the policy-holder's standpoint:

"Professor Charles K. Knight [of the Wharton School of Commerce] in discussing the ten year endowment policy, the premium of which is largely a savings payment, says: 'If the insured fails to survive the endowment period, the extra *(savings)* premium is sacrificed to the companies.'

"Even Emory McClintock, back in the days of Elizur Wright, had much the same opinion [as MacLean's, quoted above] . . . He showed that whether the savings bank theory be adopted or not, mathematically the same results followed from either theory.

"Then there is the viewpoint of the Commonwealth of Massachusetts. The Savings Bank Life Insurance Department of that state informs those about to be entrapped by the dubious Endowment policy, that 'Endowment insurance is supposedly a combination of savings and insurance, but in event of death you receive only the face of the policy. The savings part of the premium has been forfeited.'

"It seems to us that the answer to the question lies in the mind or intention of the insured. We believe the average policy-holder wants to buy an insurance policy; one that throws the risk of loss on the company. He has neither the desire nor the funds to buy a policy which gets the company off the risk as the years pass; he wants an insurance policy, not a savings contract or a combination of the two. When he buys the usual combination policy, so well described by Mr. Linton, he usually does so by reason of the inducement of apparent low cost, resulting from the grossly misleading method of estimating net cost in general use by the companies and their agents. On any fair and honest presentation of actual cost, he would probably steer clear of the combination policy.

"Mr. Linton's presentation of the matter raises several interesting questions. If the reserve or cash value is a savings balance, then it should be given the same consideration which reputable savings banks give to their savings depositors and their balances.

"If the usual policy is a combination of insurance and savings, then Mr. Linton's policy-holders will want to know why they cannot continue the insurance protection which alone is within their ability to pay for, and discontinue the now impossible savings payment; why they cannot withdraw for present needs their savings

> balance, yet continue their insurance protection.
> "This is the core of the twisting problem . . .
> The average policy-holder . . . wants to buy
> insurance-protection for his family; he believes
> his policy to be an *insurance* policy, not in part
> a savings policy. If perchance he has bought an
> impossible policy, he wants to drop the impos-
> sible part . . ."

Let us go further. After "saving" for several
years, a *second* liability, and a more subtle one, is
reflected in the ledger of your estate. If your cash
value were in a bank, or generally employed as
capital, it would earn interest for you. But when
it remains with the company, they earn the interest. Therefore, you are contributing to the
company the interest-worth of any cash value
within your policy. (And, of course, if you borrow any cash you actually pay the company
interest.)

Insurance men sometimes argue that your cash
value is (very hypothetically speaking) earning you
interest within the policy; the reserve accumulates
on a 3 or 3½ percent basis. The argument is not
important but it should be met; moreover, its consideration will illustrate the second liability.

The fact that the company adds the interest to
the cash value, in itself virtually refutes the theory
that you get any interest. We have discovered that
your cash value is a liability; at your death, it
becomes a loss. Any interest included in that cash
value is likewise forfeit. During your life, both

interest and principal are "shackled." As long as your cash remains in the policy, you contribute the amount of interest it could earn. This contribution of the interest to the company is the second liability.

The reality of these two liabilities was emphasized by Joseph B. Maclean, Assistant Actuary of the Mutual Life Insurance Company of New York, in an article that appeared in the *Eastern Underwriter,* October 7, 1927:

> "A good deal of misunderstanding in connection with twists and changes arises from the idea that the annual cost of an insurance policy is the annual premium paid. It is evident that part of the cost where the policy has a cash surrender value is represented by interest on that value. The cash value can be drawn on demand. If it were drawn, interest could be earned upon it. The company actually holds the amount of the cash value, and earns interest upon it which is not paid to the policy-holder. The insured therefore pays over the interest on his cash value just as clearly as if he held the cash value himself, earned interest upon it and paid the interest to the company. This brings out the point which is of the greatest importance in all the transactions at present under discussion, that, on the level premium plan of insurance, the amount of insurance at any time is not the face amount of the policy, but the face amount less the cash value."

These two liabilities, creation of cash value (or self-insurance) and contribution of interest, will be incurred every time you attempt to save within an insurance policy. Protect your dependents with insurance—save somewhere else.

CHAPTER FIVE

RENEWABLE TERM—YOUR MONEY'S WORTH

There is only one type policy that gives you a dollar's worth of protection for every dollar you spend. There is only one type contract that provides protection alone, and does not overcharge for a shoddy savings feature. It is the cheapest kind of insurance, costing, at age 35, less than half as much as Ordinary Life, one-third as much as 20-Payment Life, and one-fifth as much as 20-Year Endowment.

People are so apt to buy according to the yardstick of price that they refuse to buy it because the word "cheap" connotes poor quality. It is so inexpensive that the ordinary insurance-buyer, if he ever learns of its existence, suspects a trick; it looks too good to be true. His usual question is: "What's the catch?"

Agents never recommend it, and hate to sell it, because it brings them a negligible commission. Companies are loath to issue it because it creates no cash values for them to play with. Due to this conspiracy of silence, the public is scarcely aware that such a type policy is sold at all. And for those who do hear of it, special arguments have been devised to make its merits appear as drawbacks.

Only two classes of people ever buy it: those who understand insurance perfectly, and those who are so financially up against it that they cannot afford expensive insurance, thus getting their money's worth without knowing it.

This type policy is the Renewable Term Contract.

* * *

You should not save within an insurance policy. Rising mortality-costs cannot be avoided. With these two fundamental ideas clearly understood, you are ready to cope with the problem of securing the best insurance available under present conditions. The best insurance is that whose costs* rise no more than mortality-costs demand.

The policy whose rates most closely conform with mortality-costs for any age is the One-Year Renewable Term contract. This policy provides insurance-protection—nothing more. It is the cheapest form of insurance because it is divorced from any overcharge-for-saving. Its cost is the

---

* Not to be confused with premium-payments. Our later chapters will demonstrate that your actual insurance-costs in any cash value policy are usually much greater than your yearly premium.

basic cost of all the varieties of so-called life-insurance. It alone assesses for the current mortality-
cost plus overhead. That is all you should pay.
Every other type policy contains these costs, with
the addition, however, of varying amounts of overcharge.

The features of the One-Year Renewable Term
contract are:

(1) It is automatically renewable at the end of
each year, at the attained-age rate.

(2) It renews *without* a medical re-examin-
ation.

(3) It never contains cash value; it always contains the full face amount of protection.

(4) It is permanent insurance.

There are alternative Renewable Term contracts that are similar to 1-Year Renewable Term.
These plans are the 5-, 10-, 15-, and 20-Year Renewable Term policies. Instead of renewing at
the end of each year, they automatically renew at
the end of the specified period. The premium
rate does not rise from year to year, as in 1-Year
Renewable Term; it is levelled over the specified
number of years.

The 10-Year Renewable Term, for example,
requires a uniform premium-payment for ten
years. This premium is computed, roughly speaking, by averaging the 1-Year Renewable Term
premiums for the same period. At the end of the
tenth year, when the policy renews, the new rate

will be the new average—the 1-Year Renewable Term rates for the next ten years, totalled and divided by ten.

The alternative Renewable Term plans are, in all other respects, exactly like 1-Year Renewable Term, and have the same features: they renew without evidence of insurability, they never create cash value, their protection never decreases, their rates rise more or less in conformity with rising mortality-costs, and they afford permanent insurance.

And these very features of Renewable Term, which make it the most advisable form of insurance for you to buy, have been the basis for the uncritical attacks made upon it. Rising costs—and no cash values! How often have agents drummed these phrases into the credulous ears of inquirers to steer them into the higher-premium forms? And how foolishly they have succumbed!

It rarely occurs to the insured to question the agent's summary dismissal of the Renewable Term forms. Policy-holders are so accustomed to rely on the agent's familiarity with all kinds of contracts, on his supposed understanding of the merits and disadvantages of contracts, that they seldom ask for a "complete comparison" of policies. Moreover, rare is the agent who is qualified to present one.

Let us see what these "rising costs" really amount to:

ONE YEAR RENEWABLE TERM RATES*

FOR EACH $1,000 OF INSURANCE

Attained Age	Annual Premium	Attained Age	Annual Premium
21	$7.74	40	$ 9.65
22	7.79	41	9.96
23	7.84	42	10.31
24	7.89	43	10.67
25	7.95	44	11.19
26	8.01	45	11.60
27	8.08	46	12.18
28	8.15	47	12.82
29	8.22	48	13.53
30	8.30	49	14.38
31	8.38	50	15.31
32	8.48	51	16.23
33	8.60	52	17.25
34	8.70	53	18.38
35	8.82	54	19.67
36	8.96	55	21.08
37	9.10	56	22.67
38	9.27	57	24.42
39	9.45	58	26.37
..	..	59	28.55

* Wherever we must cite specific costs for Renewable Term, we will refer to the 1-Year Renewable Term rates. We do this not because we recommend that plan alone—we recommend any of them which include the four features previously mentioned—but because its rates correspond more closely to the current mortality-costs. Hence, it provides the best available indication of the basic, and irreduceable, insurance-cost for any age. The rates are quoted from a contract issued by one of the eastern life-insurance companies.

Notice how slight the increase is from year to year. Even at age 54, the cost has not equalled the premium for an Ordinary Life Policy taken out at age 35, twenty years ago! During this period, the holder of an Ordinary Life Policy would have been paying $20.06 every year. Subtracting the Renewable Term rates from that cost, you can readily see an enormous difference in favor of the Renewable Term. In the Ordinary Life policy, this difference would be represented by a theoretical cash value. But the holder of a Renewable Term contract would have the difference in his estate.

It is obvious that 1-Year Renewable Term is the cheapest insurance up to age 55. No one, including the most ignorant agent, denies that. The argument runs that after age 55, the cost mounts in bigger jumps, becoming prohibitive after age 70. And at age 95, the cost is appalling.

This argument must be treated at length. It is the argument that is used to discourage you from buying Renewable Term, and to sell you high-priced insurance.

Follow carefully. First of all, the mortality-cost for your attained age must be met, no matter what type policy you carry, or when you took it out, or how long it has been in force. This mortality-cost, which corresponds to the 1-Year Renewable Term rates, is a basic cost you must meet every year. (The analyses in later chapters will demonstrate how the companies get you to pay this basic cost without your knowing it.)

In all contracts except Renewable Term, you pay amounts far in excess of those necessary costs. It is only by juggling statistics, by sleight-of-hand with figures, that companies have been able to delude you into believing that you can avoid an increasing cost for protection as you advance in years. You cannot avoid it; this does not mean that you cannot *prepare* for it, by setting aside a reserve in your early years (when your earning power is greatest) to meet the higher mortality costs of later years. That is how the companies in their high-premium policies "avoid" for you those costs: *you* "avoid" them by paying them in advance.

LEVELLING—HOW THIS "AVOIDING" PROCESS WORKS

Originally, only Term insurance was sold. Over a period of years, the companies created the many other forms to assist you to prepare for higher costs for insurance in the advanced ages. They devised the "Level Premium Plans". The purpose is excellent—their device is damnable.

A levelling process is not complicated. You pay a uniform premium throughout life, rather than one which starts low and slowly rises as mortality costs demand. By paying more than mortality costs in the early years, you create a reserve (or cash value) in your policy. Then, *if you live,* and the mortality costs rise to a point where they exceed the uniform premium, the reserve is drawn upon to supply the necessary difference.

But so great are the overcharges, so rapidly does your reserve accumulate, that when the mortality cost begins to exceed the premium, the interest on your large cash reserve is more than sufficient to cover the necessary increase. And actually your reserve never decreases; it keeps growing despite its partial use for mortality-costs. In time, the reserve reaches a point where it equals the face amount of the policy. The Ordinary Life policy, for example, endows itself at age 96—the company returns your reserve or self-insurance to you. Their obligation ceases. *You have paid your own death claim.* And if you die at any age before 96, the reserve you have built up to prepare for future mortality costs is used to help pay your death claim.

Therefore, under this contract, the longer you live the more you contribute toward your own death claim.

In his text book Life Insurance, Professor S. S. Huebner, says the following:

"But keeping the premium the same from year to year, instead of increasing it in accordance with increasing age, involves the payment during the earlier years of a sum over and above that required to pay the current cost of insurance. In

> other words during the early years the company
> is accumulating a fund out of excess premiums
> which will be drawn upon in the later years
> when the same annual premium becomes insuf-
> ficient to meet the current cost. This overcharge
> in the yearly premiums does not belong to the
> company but is held in trust for the policy-
> holder at an assumed rate of interest for the
> purpose just indicated."

That is, you are saving within your policy, you
are building a reserve which might never be
needed. With the present set-up, any attempt at
saving succeeds in decreasing the amount of net
protection in your policy. For they apply your
reserve toward settling your policy when it matures
as a death claim. As we have stated, your reserve
becomes self-insurance. And to the extent that
you co-insure yourself, you decrease the amount
of protection in your policy.

Thus, under levelling plans, you are really making two payments: one for this year's mortality
cost, and another for mortality costs of later years.
You are buying first, present protection, and at
the same time you are saving up a sum to be used
for future protection. It should be understood
that, in many ways, it would be to your advantage
to treat these items independently; to keep your
future-protection program divorced from your
present-protection program. If you keep the two
separated, at death the unused portion of the invested sum (if you do not have a long life, none

of it may be used) will revert to your estate, along with the full face amount of protection. At present, when the investment is wrapped up with insurance, the investment-fund becomes merely part of the death claim, or, if you prefer, is forfeited.

In other words, the companies could keep a double ledger with policy-holders who want to pay on a level premium basis. One page of this double account would be devoted to payments for present protection on a Renewable Term basis, and the other page to the excess payments which may never be needed. With this double ledger, if you die before you fulfill the purpose of your savings (the payment for high Term premiums in the extreme later years), the amount of your savings or excess payments would be returned *in addition* to the full face amount of protection you purchased and paid for.

Sheppard Homans, compiler of the American Experience Table of Mortality, an actuary who completely understood insurance and its function, appreciated the advisability of the foregoing more than sixty years ago!   He said:

> "There is but one function for the institution of life insurance and that is protection. There is but one form of contract issued by a legal reserve company that will give the insured a square deal. The companies are introducing a [savings] feature which, while it increases the

cost of insurance, does not increase the protection. Therefore, the companies should be compelled to open a double entry account with each policy-holder. Then, in event of the insured dying before the investment part of his contract became effective, the company would be compelled to return to the beneficiary, in addition to the face of the policy, that amount he had placed with the company for a purpose he had failed to live to realize."

What is this "form of contract" whose only function is protection, the contract that "will give the insured a square deal," the policy that is not combined with a dubious savings-feature?

It is the Renewable Term contract—the policy that contains only insurance-protection, and whose costs rise no more than mortality-costs warrant.

Levelling can be an *individual* process. You can, if you wish, prepare for the rising mortality-costs of as many later years as you think necessary. Your levelling need not be dependent upon or influenced by the levelling of some other policy-holder's payments. Once you pay your mortality-costs for the current year—represented by the Renewable Term premium—any arrangement you make, necessitating accumulations for future purposes, can be an individual matter, regulated according to your income. These accumulations will not go into a company mortuary fund but into an outside reserve that will be your real savings. They will be diverted into the mortuary fund only if you live to that advanced age when the annual outlay you previously decided to make becomes insufficient to meet your mortality-cost for that year. If you die before that time, your estate will gain the full amount of accumulated savings; no portion of the outside reserve will be used or needed to make up your death claim. The companies can meet every obligation with the Renewable Term premiums; your estate may suffer if you pay more.

Another disadvantageous feature of the companies' levelling method consists in that they level your premium payments to cover the mortality-costs to age 96. By way of a justification for this practice, the companies cite the American Experience Table of Mortality. Out of the hundred thousand people chosen, three actually did live to ninety-six. Any policy-holder might conceivably be one of these three. Therefore, every policy-holder takes an undue risk if he doesn't prepare to meet the mortality-cost for that extreme age.

We do not like to insult the reader's intelligence. But, for all we know, there may possibly be one reader who does not catch the fallacy. For his benefit—and for his alone—we will point it out. Assume that three do live. Can they by any stretch of the imagination need or want insurance at 96? The purpose of insurance, you will remember, is to protect dependents. It seems reasonable to suppose that the children of a nonagen-

arian will be boys big enough to fend for themselves. (And if they cannot, they can fall back
on old-age pensions.) If you should die at age
95 without insurance, what a terrible financial
blow that would be to your little Willie—a wee
lad of seventy dependent upon you for support!

There is an ancient story about a census taker
who chanced upon a 90-year old gentleman play-
ing marbles in his front yard. "How many are in
your family?" he asked.

The marble-shooting gentleman looked up. "I
don't know," he said, "I'm the baby of the family.
Daddy is up in his airplane. But when grandpop
comes in from roller-skating, you can ask him."
Levelled life insurance was made expressly for that
family.

Some companies, in the bitter competition for
business, have issued Term Expectancy contracts.
These are levelled to your expectancy age, rather
than to age 96. Hence, the level payments ($14.95
at age 35) are much lower than those of the
Ordinary Life contract ($20.06 at the same age).
It is a move in the right direction. Next to Renewable Term, it best meets the needs of the insuring public.

Facing is the American Experience Table which
shows the expectation of life at any given age. A
man age 35, for example, may expect to live an
average of 31.78 more years; hence, his expectancy
is between 66 and 67. Refer to the Table to de-

THE AMERICAN EXPERIENCE TABLE OF MORTALITY

Age	Expect. of Life in Yrs.	No. Dying each 1000	Age	Expect. of Life in Yrs.	No. Dying each 1000	Age	Expect. of Life in Yrs.	No. Dying each 1000
20	42.20	7.81	46	23.81	11.56	71	8.00	67.67
21	41.53	7.86	47	23.08	12.00	72	7.55	73.73
22	40.85	7.91	48	22.36	12.51	73	7.11	80.18
23	40.17	7.96	49	21.63	13.11	74	6.68	87.03
24	39.49	8.01	50	20.91	13.78	75	6.27	94.37
25	38.81	8.07	51	20.20	14.54	76	5.88	102.31
26	38.12	8.13	52	19.49	15.39	77	5.49	111.06
27	37.43	8.20	53	18.79	16.33	78	5.11	120.83
28	36.73	8.26	54	18.09	17.40	79	4.74	131.73
29	36.03	8.35	55	17.40	18.57	80	4.39	144.47
30	35.33	8.43	56	16.72	19.89	81	4.05	158.61
31	34.63	8.51	57	16.05	21.34	82	3.71	174.30
32	33.92	8.61	58	15.39	22.94	83	3.39	191.56
33	33.21	8.72	59	14.74	24.72	84	3.08	211.36
34	32.50	8.83	60	14.10	26.69	85	2.77	235.55
35	31.78	8.95	61	13.47	28.88	86	2.47	265.68
36	31.07	9.09	62	12.86	31.29	87	2.18	303.02
37	30.35	9.23	63	12.26	33.94	88	1.91	346.69
38	29.62	9.41	64	11.67	36.87	89	1.66	395.86
39	28.90	9.59	65	11.10	40.13	90	1.42	454.55
40	28.18	9.79	66	10.54	43.71	91	1.19	532.47
41	27.45	10.01	67	10.00	47.65	92	.98	634.26
42	26.72	10.25	68	9.47	52.00	93	.80	734.18
43	26.00	10.52	69	8.97	56.76	94	.64	857.14
44	25.27	10.83	70	8.48	61.99	95	.50	1000.00
45	24.54	11.16	..	..	..	..	..	....

termine the average expectation of life for your age.

Assuredly, it is wise to create reserves, but keep them separate from your insurance-protection. The accumulations would thus be available to you at all times, free of any "shackles." These shackles are applicable whether you regard the excess payments made to the company as savings or as a reserve for future mortality-costs. From the practical point-of-view, therefore, the two viewpoints concerning the reserve are identical. Accordingly, you have no alternative but to buy Renewable Term and, if you wish, do your own levelling.

RENEWABLE TERM—AND ESTATE PLANNING

You bought insurance in the first place to leave a lump sum of money or an income to your family in the event of your premature death; in the second place, to save systematically so that, if you live, you will be financially independent in old-age. You now realize the futility of trying to accomplish this two-fold plan with insurance. The way to succeed in doing both is to create a saving-and-investment program outside insurance, and a protection program through insurance.

The first problem in planning your estate is to determine the income or lump sum you want to leave your dependents during their dependency period. It is not your intention or obligation to

support your children after they become self-supporting. Hence, it is of the utmost importance
to procure the maximum of protection while your
needs are greatest—a truism so simple that it is
usually overlooked. If your family now consists,
say, of your widowed mother, your wife, and three
children, you probably need more insurance now
than at any subsequent period in your life. With
Renewable Term, you can afford to carry an
adequate amount of protection now. In twenty
years, your Renewable Term rate will be higher—
but you will need less insurance: your total insurance-cost will, in all probability, be much
smaller. For when your mother dies, it is point-
less to continue to carry the insurance you bought
to protect her; you can safely drop that much insurance, eliminating its cost. In a similar manner,
you can reduce your insurance program when a
son becomes self-supporting or a daughter marries
(or if either dies). By the time your rate-per-
thousand for Renewable Term rises to a point
where it is supposed to be "burdensome," your
total insurance bill, to judge from the experience
of others, will be considerably less than it was
when the rates were low. The chances are that
your sole dependent will be your wife, assuming
that she is alive. (Writers on life insurance, like
undertakers, must at times appear to have a morbid
pre-occupation with death.) Never let the bug-
aboo of "rising costs" frighten you; along with

"rising costs" go decreasing needs, hence lower total costs.

If you are to follow any sensible program, you want the maximum protection when you need it the most. With Renewable Term, you enter into no pseudo-saving plan that creates liabilities for your estate. There is nothing, however, to prevent you from saving outside your policies. That is up to you. For those who wish to save, we will consider an elaboration of the foregoing plan.

Let us assume that your dependents need an annual income of $5,000. Your insurance company, in its advertisements and educational literature, might lead you to believe that, in order to provide this amount for your family in the event of your death, you would need an insurance estate of $100,000. At five percent, the interest earned on this amount would leave them an income of $5,000 a year.

This is only part of the truth. After the death of your dependents, what is to become of the interest on the $100,000? Shall it go on forever, to provide for generations still unborn? Can you afford to leave a $5,000 income to eternity? And what is finally to become of the $100,000 principal?

When we recall the terrific lapse-rate, nine policies out of ten never reaching maturity, we must conclude that too many policy-holders have tried to do the impossible. Your obligation to your dependents virtually stops when you have attained your expectancy age.   You can learn your expectation of life by referring to the Mortality Table facing page 84.   The Table has its limitations but it presents as correct a forecast as we need for our present purpose.   Another table which might aid you in determining your chance of living is supplied by the U. S. Bureau of Census:

Only 51.6% of the people now alive are over 25 years of age
Only 16.5% of the people now alive are over 50 years of age
Only 8.6% of the people now alive are over 60 years of age
Only 5.8% of the people now alive are over 65 years of age
Only 3.8% of the people now alive are over 70 years of age
Only   .5% of the people now alive are over 80 years of age

Let us take up your first purpose; to provide your family with an income of, say, $5,000, until your expectancy age (which at age 35, is 67), in the event of your death before that time.   How much insurance is needed to create this income?   Obviously, using the interest and part of the principal each year, a much smaller original lump sum than $100,000, will provide the $5,000 income to your expectancy age.

And at age 45 you will need considerably less insurance than you needed at age 35.   This is because you now have ten years' income less to provide for.   Since you lived those ten years and supplied the income from your annual earnings, it is unnecessary for you to duplicate that income with your insurance.   Therefore, from year to year, as you yourself provide income, you can drop the amount of insurance you bought to serve that purpose if you had died. In other words, the plan requires that amount of protection which will be necessary to supply the same income which you would have supplied had you lived.

As you drop the insurance you no longer need, you avoid the higher mortality-cost in the later years for that amount. Not only do you avoid the costs, but by not attempting to support countless generations, you can really fulfill your program for your immediate dependents, and avoid the consequences which usually follow when you bite off more than you can chew.

Any good plan calls for the purchase of the best insurance-protection you can get—Renewable Term. Since this is the lowest-cost insurance it obviously will release an enormous difference in the size of your premium payments. The utilization of this difference remains up to you; you can spend it as you make it, or you can save it and apply the interest to pay for anything you wish. If you save it as part of your estate, you will soon reach a point where the interest on the savings is sufficient to pay for your insurance-protection.

Very shortly then, if you wish to save this difference, the estate can be made self-supporting. Moreover, this saving, being outside your policy, reverts to your estate—and not to the insurance company—at death. Also this saving will speed up the process of eliminating the need for insurance.

For example, as you save $1,000, you can drop a thousand dollars worth of insurance—since the savings would really go to your estate. Hence, as you save on the outside, you constantly need less insurance to accomplish your original purpose.

You know that increased mortality-costs cannot be avoided if you carry insurance in the later years. The plan above is a practical method of avoiding those higher costs. For only by eliminating the need for insurance, can you eliminate the cost for insurance. With Renewable Term, you get insurance in the early years at a low rate, and if you follow this plan, you don't need any insurance when the rates get high.

An intelligent savings plan calls for the identical principles employed by the life insurance companies—but with the methods reversed. That is, you still have a cash reserve, but it is outside the policy, in your possession. By reversing the method, you gain what the companies have been gaining at your expense.

Moreover, if you buy Renewable Term to *replace your present insurance,* and afterward surrender the latter insurance for its cash value (automatically cancelling all loans) you manifestly effect a great saving. The cash you retrieve would make a fine beginning for your outside saving-fund. In fact, the interest you earn on this retrieved cash may be enough to pay for your new low-rate insurance.

When men connected with life insurance companies attack this plan, they are compelled to resort to a shallow, irrelevant argument. First they demonstrate that if the savings-fund outside the policy is accumulating at a very low rate of interest, it will grow less rapidly than the theoretical cash value in a policy. Therefore, runs their conclusion, it is better for the insured to save within his insurance contract.

The fallacy is almost self-evident. Making a comparison between the represented amount of money in the cash value and the real amount of money in an outside saving-fund is meaningless. Whether one is greater or less than the other—which depends upon the rate of interest the money outside can earn—has practically no bearing. A true comparison would point out that the cash value is shackled during the life of the policyholder, and is retained by the company at his death; while the outside savings are his to use at any time unshackled, and go to his beneficiary when he dies.

This brings out the important point that the policy-holder who saves within his policy has a *stationary* estate: the maximum he can ever leave his beneficiary is the face amount of the policy. The possessor of an outside saving-fund, on the other hand, has a constantly *growing* estate. Regardless of which one saves faster, it is evident that the latter increases the size of his estate with every savings deposit; the former merely decreases the amount of net insurance in his policy: the size of his total estate—insurance plus cash value—always remains the same. As a matter of fact, there is an exception to the "always." Assume that each policy-holder has a $10,000 policy. The first, with a cash-value policy, has accumulated $4,000 within the policy; the other, with a Renewable Term policy, has accumulated $4,000 in an outside fund. Both meet financial setbacks and are forced to avail themselves of all ready cash. Now get the picture: the first must borrow on his policy, must pay six percent interest annually ($240), and furthermore has reduced his estate to $6,000. The other simply withdraws his outside savings and still has an estate of $10,000. Only an incomplete comparison, a misrepresentation of facts, can "prove" that protection and savings should be combined. The full comparison, as we have outlined it, in itself demonstrates the hollowness of the argument sponsored by the companies.

Another sophism advanced by company-subsidized "experts," and immeasurably more stupid than the preceding one, is that "the Average Man can not save systematically." Unless he is compelled by the terms of his policy to save within his policy, he will not save at all. So, although the actuarial methods employed by the company require him to forfeit his savings at death, there is no harm done: the thriftless Average Man would

not have saved on the outside anyway—which
would leave the beneficiary deprived in either case.
Here is absurdity on horseback, yet many insurance apologists have submitted it to the authors
in all seriousness.   Only in extremely rare cases
can a life insurance company compel you to save.
The alarmingly high lapse-rate for "saving-and-
protection" policies furnishes conclusive evidence
that the compulsion is inadequate.   Provided you
have the will to save, and provided you have the
necessary income, you will save.   If these two provisions are absent, then insurance contracts, Building and Loan Shares, or Christmas Club plans will
have little noticeable effect.

The "forced saving" argument is—and this is
the important point—not merely stupid but
vicious.   To understand its harmfulness, it is
necessary to consider the difference between the
needs served by protection and by savings.   Most
men need both; upon this fact the companies base
their whole claim to the right of selling both of
them in one contract.   What they fail to mention
is that protection is a *present* and *constant* need
which must be provided for immediately; savings,
on the other hand—whether it be destined to
supply an income in old age or to take care of
rising mortality-costs in the later years—is not a
pressing, immediate need; provision for it may be
deferred to a time in the future.

To make it plainer, let us suppose that you

have a "Retirement Income Policy," a contract which combines a small amount of protection with a large amount of "savings." When the agent sold it to you, he stressed the savings element and pointed out that, by compelling you to save systematically along with your protection, the policy would enable you to achieve financial independence at your retirement age. Well and good. But the premiums are high and your income is just sufficient for you to pay them. Now, suppose that the present year is a slack one in your business; your income falls to a point where you must seriously retrench. Where would a sane man begin economizing? Obviously not on food, or shelter, or on his children's education. Obviously not on his insurance-protection—which he needs today more than ever. He would want to cut down, first of all, on his savings, putting less aside this year than usual. Rather than forego a present necessity, he would prefer even to skip this year's saving or postpone it, since it is intended to take care of a need far in the future, a need which might never materialize. According to your contract, however, you cannot do this without running into the "shackles" we spoke of in Chapter Four. You cannot avoid the stipulated annual expenditure for savings unless you are willing to sacrifice your insurance. Most policy-holders, whether they happen to be willing or not, find that the companies' "forced saving plan" becomes a forced

lapse-or-surrender plan. When the savings part
of the contract becomes impossible to continue,
the protection part must also be discontinued.

This is a major disadvantage—not of savings in
itself, but of the combination of savings and protection in the same contract. If the two were kept
separate, the insured would have complete mobility
at all times. Any unforeseen contingency—business reverses, prolonged sickness in the family,
unemployment, to name but a few—may make it
unfeasible for you to save during any one year.
With savings kept apart from protection, the omis-
sion is not irreparable. If circumstances prevent
you from saving this year, you can make it up next
year—or three years from now.

But regardless of whether your saving is rigidly
systematic, if you do want to save, you can see how
Renewable Term facilitates it. By employing Renewable Term and saving the difference between
its cost and the cost for the usual "savings" policy,
you will in time endow yourself and have no need
for insurance. You will have created an actual
fund which, if (amortized using the interest earned
and part of the principal) will provide a substantial income for you in later years. Should you
die before the entire fund is amortized, it would
revert to your beneficiaries.

It is of vital importance to remember that there
are Term Contracts which are *not* renewable. Do
not confuse these with the Renewable plans. Some

companies do not sell Renewable Term contracts; never let an agent persuade you to buy a Term policy which does not renew for as long as you think necessary. Non-Renewable Term, and Term that must shortly be converted into some other form, both serve important purposes; but they do not represent permanent, inexpensive insurance.

Never forget that there are Renewable types which are *permanent* insurance. Once you pass the physical examination and have secured such a policy, you can keep yourself insured as long as it is necessary, without further evidence of insurability. The lowered costs you pay for these contracts, releasing large sums of money for other purposes, will be reflected in an increased estate. If you use the difference for true saving, and let it earn real interest for you, the money you might have wasted for high-priced insurance becomes an asset—and not a liability. In this way you do not become co-insurer of your own protection, and you do not contribute the interest that is rightfully yours. It is worth mentioning that, if you are one who needs more protection, you could probably double your insurance estate with your present insurance costs.

Another point, of incalculable importance to your dependents. Never will you find it necessary, or possible, with these Renewable Term plans to sacrifice their protection to salvage your savings.

You have recognized the necessity of separating savings from protection.

It takes courage to go counter to the propaganda of companies, the selfishness of agents, and the advice of uninformed friends. But equipped with the fundamental principles of insurance, you will be capable of independent judgment. You will have no reason to be swayed by the opinions of others. Renewable Term answers everyone's "insurance need." Most policy-holders who now have Renewable Term cannot afford any other type of insurance. Desperate financial straits forced them to eliminate insurance-wastes—or go without insurance altogether. Must you wait until adverse circumstances force you to buy insurance intelligently? The fact that you have money is no reason to squander it in insurance orgies. There are more enjoyable ways of wasting money . . .

CHAPTER SIX

DIVIDENDS: THE "MUTUAL" MYTH

Let us continue our treatment of what insurance is not. We have demonstrated that insurance is not a good method of saving. It is also not a method of investment. The widespread belief that life insurance is an investment institution arises from the peculiar workings of the so-called "Mutual" companies.

Life insurance companies can be broadly classified into two types: the Mutual—which issues Participating policies; and the Stock company—which issues Non-Participating policies.

According to popular faith, the Mutual companies pay dividends—which implies that a Participating policy is an investment. The policy-holder in these companies is led, by the concerted effort of company and agent, to believe that he is sharing in the profits of the company.

Forever rid yourself of that misconception. The "dividend" checks you get have no similarity to dividends from a genuine investment. For the "dividends" the policy-holder collects from the Mutual company are his own money. Every policy taken out in a Participating company requires a larger premium than the same policy in a Non-Participating company. Having charged you more for the Participating policy, the Mutual company subsequently returns part of your overpayment and calls it a "dividend."

Such "dividends" are only partial refunds on overcharges that never should have been made in the first place.

They have nothing to do with the cash value in your policy. The Aetna Life Insurance Company of Connecticut and the Philadelphia Life Insurance Company, to take two examples, sell both Participating and Non-Participating policies, with equal cash values in both. Agents and companies are forbidden by law to predict the probable return. Hence, "dividends" are not guaranteed. The "dividends" you hope to get may or may not approximate the amount which you overpay for "participating." And you always face the possibility of getting no return at all—as has happened in the past.

S. S. Huebner, in *The Principles of Life Insurance,* a book "Endorsed by the Education and Conservation Bureau of the National Association of Life Underwriters," has the following to say about "dividends":

"In actual practice, therefore, the stock company charges a lower rate of premium on non-participating policies than does the mutual company on participating policies. The stock company says in effect, to quote one description, 'keep the dividend (of the mutual company) in your pocket.' It follows the plan of discounting the future—i. e., of paying its dividends in advance—by charging a guaranteed low premium; while the mutual company asks a higher premium to start with and subsequently refunds the overcharges."

Notice, he plainly states that they give back only overcharges. The returns ("dividends") you may get from the Mutual company are not likely to equal for ten years or more, the amount the Non-Participating company leaves in your pocket in the first place. *And, remember, the life of the average policy is seven years.*

The foregoing views are substantiated by every actuary. Joseph B. Maclean, Assistant Actuary of the *Mutual* Life Insurance Company, in his book *Life Insurance,* concurs:

"It will be seen that the word 'dividend' is a misnomer, the 'dividend' being rather in the nature of a refund and not a return on investment as the term is generally used in commercial transactions."

Mr. Maclean knows the truth about "dividends." We wonder how many policy-holders in Mr. Maclean's company know it. Certainly, not many.

The majority of policies are Participating; practically all the large companies are Mutual. The average policy-holder has never seen Non-Participating rates. Rare, indeed, is the policy-holder who has had the opportunity of comparing them with Participating rates. Yet, it is an instructive comparison:

PREMIUM RATES (AT AGE 35) FOR $10,000 PARTICIPATING AND NON-PARTICIPATING POLICIES

	Ordinary Life	20-Payment Life	20-Year Endowment
Participating	$281.10	$383.40	$519.10
Non-Participating	200.60	278.20	420.90
Overpayment for Participating in "Dividends"	$ 80.50	$105.20	$ 98.20

Even a cursory examination of the above comparison reveals that the "dividends" must be generously apportioned to equal the annual overpayment for dividends. Many holders of Participating policies, unaware of the lower Non-Participating rates, would gladly forego "dividends" and would spend the cost-differential for more insurance if they knew the truth about "dividends." In the Ordinary Life policy, for example, the $80-overpayment is large enough to procure an additional $4,000 policy.

However, when you think of buying or dropping insurance, don't let the "dividends" influence you too much.   Actually, over a long period of years, the costs for both types tend to equal each other. Of course, with the Participating type, an early death means sacrifice of the overpayments-for-dividends.   The guaranteed plans of the Non-Participating companies are, in our opinion, more desirable—in view of the limited life of the average policy.

But in this chapter we are interested more in exploding the myth of "dividends" than in recommending Non-Participating policies. Bear in mind, though, that the overcharge-for-dividends has nothing to do with the overcharge which creates cash value.   The savings overcharge is present equally in both Participating and Non-Participating types, and builds up the same liabilities.

In our future chapters, in which we analyze policies, we use Non-Participating contracts only. Our purpose is to simplify the analyses.   The inclusion of "dividends," which have relatively little bearing on your real costs, would succeed only in complicating the subject.   As you read such analyses, keep in mind that they apply with equal force to Participating contracts.

Two Kinds of Insurance

Insurance policies may be broadly classified into two further types.

(1) Those in which you create no self-insurance,

and in which the protection never decreases, remaining constant from year to year. Such policies are the Renewable Term contracts.

(2) Those in which you co-insure yourself, decreasing the net protection in the policy from year to year. Typical examples are Ordinary Life, Limited Payment Life, and Endowment policies.

In the next few chapters, we will examine and analyze these undesirable contracts, employing the principles we have developed in the preceding chapters.

CHAPTER SEVEN

WHAT AN ORDINARY LIFE POLICY
REALLY COSTS

You now have a theoretical understanding of the principles of life insurance. You know what it is—protection. And you know what it is not—investment. You should by now appreciate the futility of attempting saving within your insurance policy.

Our analysis has proved this, and its truth was confirmed by the various unbiased quotations from competent men. Many of your former misconceptions have already been shattered. Or, if not shattered, you have at least a healthy doubt which only awaits further proof to complete the job.

We will examine together the Ordinary Life Policy,* one of the most popular forms sold. We will not be content to note the mere premium charges, but will seek to discover the true costs you pay for this form.

We shall go with you to buy a $10,000 Ordinary Life Policy at age 35. The agent joyfully assures

———
*Often called "Whole Life," or "Straight Life."

you that you are getting the cheapest form of permanent protection; that the initial premium sets the rate for the rest of your life; that hence, you avoid the increasing mortality-costs of later years. He stresses that you are, moreover, embarking upon a systematic saving plan which will create a cash value which is yours at any time for the asking (*sic!*).

We will not take time now to point out that most agents are amazingly ignorant of the fundamentals of life insurance, and that those who are not ignorant are usually shrewd ballyhoo-merchants. That, we reserve for a special chapter. Let us proceed at once to examine the actual conditions that will develop in the Ordinary Life Policy you are buying.

Non-Participating Ordinary Life Policy

(see page facing)

What do the various columns mean?

Notice that under "Cash Value," the amount progressively grows higher. We explained, you recall, that this money represents your overpayments to prepare for future mortality-costs. Under the column "Extended Term Insurance," (an option included in all policies of this type), the company frankly confesses, in years and days, the extent of your accumulated overpayments. That is, if you wish to stop paying premiums when you

CURRENT-COST ANALYSIS OF ORDINARY LIFE POLICY
(NON-PARTICIPATING—TAKEN OUT AT AGE 35)

Age	Year	Face Amount of Policy	Cash Value	Net Risk to Company or Actual Protection	Premium	Interest Contributed on Cash Value at 6%	Actual Cost for Net Risk	Extended Term Insurance Yrs.	Days	Actual Cost per Thousand	1-Year Renewable Term Rates
35	1	$10,000 —	None	= $10,000.00	$200.60 +	None =	= $200.06	—	—	$ 20.06	$ 8.82
39	5	10,000 —	$ 418.20	= 9,581.80	200.60 +	$ 25.09 =	225.69	4	215	23.55	9.45
44	10	10,000 —	1,112.60	= 8,887.40	200.60 +	55.63 =	256.23	12	—	28.89	11.19
49	15	10,000 —	2,191.50	= 7,808.50	200.60 +	131.49 =	332.09	15	23	42.52	14.38
52	18	10,000 —	2,733.10	= 7,266.90	200.60 +	163.99 =	364.59	15	184	50.17	17.25
54	20	10,000 —	3,107.50	= 6,892.50	200.60 +	186.45 =	387.05	15	187	56.15	19.67
59	25	10,000 —	4,073.00	= 5,927.00	200.60 +	244.38 =	444.98	14	320	75.07	28.55
64	30	10,000 —	5,047.11	= 4,952.89	200.60 +	302.83 =	503.43	13	261	101.64	42.76

are age 49, your overpayments will carry the face amount of the policy for an additional fifteen years and twenty-three days.

Therefore, when you leave your cash with the company, regardless of whether it is through lapse or while the insurance is in force, that cash value represents a "single lump sum premium." It is as if you had purchased a pure term policy for the length of time indicated in the "Extended" column, paying for it in advance. Suppose you die one year after. What becomes of the premiums you paid in advance for the other fourteen years? You bought fifteen years of protection and received only one year's.

Again, the cash value represents the extent to which you have become co-insurer of your own estate: in the 15th year, almost 22% of the face amount of the policy. At your death, the company will not return these savings. It will apply them toward paying your death claim. That is, in this case, when the company has your overpayments amounting to $2,191.50 (your cash value), its net risk is only $7,808.50. This is all the insurance your premium is securing in the 15th year. Did the agent tell *that* to you?

The column called "Interest Contributed," represents the interest lost to your estate by leaving the cash in the policy. Although we have headed this column, "Interest Contributed," the interest will actually be paid in cases where the cash has been borrowed.

Since 6% is the customary charge levied by the companies we have used this interest factor in all our analyses. Moreover, despite the sad state of investments today, money is worth 6% or more to most businessmen. Paying off mortgages, repaying bank loans, anticipating and discounting bills, and many other uses of money can realize at least 6%. We are well aware that many people cannot get 6% on their money. But so many policy-holders have loans on their cash values, that we would only confuse you by using one rate for the interest paid on cash borrowed and another for the cash still in the policy. The whole question of the size of the interest factor is not important, as we pointed out earlier. It is important to bear in mind that money left with the company does earn interest and that that interest is contributed to the company (refer to Maclean's statement on page 70).

To discover your actual costs at any year, you add to the premium the amount of interest contributed; the total will represent your real costs for the amount of insurance entitled, "Net Risk to Company." Then divide the amount at risk into that cost, and the result will be your cost-per-thousand of insurance for this Ordinary Life policy for that year.

For example, when the policy is eighteen years old, the face amount of your policy is still $10,000. Your cash value is $2,733.10, which means you are a co-insurer to the extent of over 27% of the face amount. Therefore, the net risk to the company is only $7,266.90. The interest (on your cash accumulation) which you contribute is $163.99. Your premium is still $200.60. Adding the latter two figures, you find an actual cost of $364.59 for the net protection of $7,266.90. *This protection is therefore costing you $50.17 per thousand in the 18th year. Notice in the next column under the "Renewable Term" Plan the rate for insurance at that age is only $17.25 per thousand.* At this rate, ($17.25) your present costs could buy you an insurance estate of $21,135. Add this to the cash you retrieve if you cancel the old policy and you have an estate of $23,868.10 as compared to your present estate of $10,000. (Obviously, we are not advocating a change such as this one. Buy the amount of insurance you need. We cite this illustration merely as a yardstick to reveal the extent of your overpayments.)

In all the figures that the agent cited when selling you this type policy, did he ever mention the above facts? He advised you to buy such a policy to avoid the slowly-rising natural premium rates reflected in the Renewable Term Policies. Well, *did* you avoid them? You were duped. Compare the actual cost in any year to the cost of Renewable Term Insurance in the same year.

We have demonstrated that your Ordinary Life Policy is not what the agents and companies say it is—"inexpensive" protection.   It is actually, compared to Renewable Term, a costly insurance.

Our next two chapters will deal with popular policies that are even more expensive than Ordinary Life.   When you read them, you will understand the cardinal truth of life insurance: THE MORE YOU PAY FOR LIFE INSURANCE, THE LESS YOU RECEIVE IN ACTUAL PROTECTION.

CHAPTER EIGHT

WHY A TWENTY-PAYMENT LIFE POLICY IS NEVER "PAID-UP"

Not content with the overcharges existing in the Ordinary Life policy, the companies have devised the Limited Payment Plans. The Ordinary Life contract was bad; the Limited Payment policies are so misleading, so much more costly, that the Ordinary Life policy will seem virtuous by comparison.

Yet it is one of the best sellers. Company and agent have thought up such eloquent and persuasive arguments in its favor that the most intelligent businessmen flock to buy it. Not one man in ten thousand can see through its glaring fallacies and inordinate overcharges.

You will buy a $10,000 Twenty-Payment Life policy at age 35. Again, you are interested in the premium-payments not in themselves, but rather as they determine the actual costs you and your estate will pay.

To sell you this policy, the agent tells you that you pay premiums for only twenty years, and that from then on you have $10,000 of protection throughout life—"and no more paying." Of course, he admits, it will be necessary to pay more in those twenty years than the real cost of insurance. But these overpayments will create a large amount of savings. This saving will accumulate so that at the end of twenty years it will be large enough ($5,661.50) to pay the cost of your insurance for the rest of your life—right on through, in fact, to age 96. Moreover, he adds, this saving is always available to you for the asking. And, as one rate book puts it, ". . . if premiums are required throughout the whole of life, they will become burdensome." You don't want to go on making premium-payments all your life, do you? In later years (perhaps even before 96), your income may be reduced, you may lose your job or become incapacitated. The wisest course is to get all your payments over with, while you can afford them. Then you can sit back, confident in your security. Therefore, the agent sums up, you pay for twenty years only, you have $10,000 protection for the rest of your life, and you have a large amount of savings on tap.

So convincing is the sales-talk, so overwhelming is the slogan "All Paid-up in Twenty Years," that you can't resist. You buy the policy, as have millions of others.

Let us examine your gold brick. Our analysis will be much like the one in the previous chapter. But even more forcibly will it drive home the dic-

CURRENT-COST ANALYSIS OF 20-PAYMENT LIFE POLICY

(NON-PARTICIPATING—TAKEN OUT AT AGE 35)

Age	Year	Face Amount of Policy	Cash Value	Net Risk to Company or Actual Protection	Premium	Interest Contributed on Cash Value at 6%	Actual Cost for Net Risk	Extended Term Insurance Yrs.	Extended Term Insurance Days	Actual Cost per Thousand	1-Year Renewable Term Rates
35	1	$10,000 —	None =	$10,000.00	$278.20 +	None =	$278.20			$27.82	$ 8.82
39	5	10,000 —	$ 810.10 =	9,189.90	278.20 +	$48.61 =	326.81	9	68	35.56	9.45
44	10	10,000 —	2,076.90 =	7,923.10	278.20 +	124.61 =	402.81	18	208	50.83	11.19
49	15	10,000 —	3,840.20 =	6,159.80	278.20 +	230.41 =	508.61	25	71	82.56	14.38
54	20	10,000 —	5,661.50 =	4,338.50	278.20 +	339.69 =	617.89	Supposedly		142.42	19.67
55	21	10,000 —	5,781.30 =	4,218.70	No	346.88 =	346.88	"Paid-Up"		82.22	21.08
59	25	10,000 —	6,269.20 =	3,730.80	More	376.15 =	376.15			170.83	28.55
64	30	10,000 —	6,882.40 =	3,117.60	Premiums	412.94 =	412.94			132.44	42.76

tum: *The more you pay for life insurance, the less protection you get, and the greater are the liabilities you create for your estate.*

Carefully examine the chart opposite.

Analyzing the Ordinary Life policy in the last chapter, we discovered that in the fifteenth year your insurance was costing you at a rate of $42.52 per thousand. What is it with the Twenty-Payment Life Contract?

Under the column "Cash Value," for the fifteenth year, we find the amount of $3,840.20. With this plan, you are a co-insurer at this stage for that sum of money—more than 38 percent of the face amount of the policy.

In the "Extended Term Insurance" column, the company tells you that, in the fifteenth year of the contract, your overpayments will carry the policy for an additional twenty-five years and seventy-one days. You paid for this in advance. Were you to die at this time, your estate would lose those advanced payments.

The "Net Risk to Company" in the fifteenth year is only $6,159.80. What is your actual cost for this amount of protection? The column "Interest Contributed"—representing the interest lost to your estate by leaving the cash in the policy—shows at this time the amount of $230.41. Adding this amount to your premium of $278.20, you get the actual cost for your net protection. It is costing your estate $508.61 for $6,159.80 worth of pro-

tection. To calculate your cost-per-thousand, it
will be recalled, you divide the cost for the net
protection by the amount of net protection. For
this 20-payment Life policy, in the fifteenth year,
your rate-per-thousand is $82.56. Compare this
rate with the cost for One-Year Renewable Term
at the same age; you will discover the extent of the
deception perpetrated upon you.

In the twentieth year, when insurance is pur-
chasable for $19.67 per thousand, the chart shows
an actual cost of $142.42!

So in this contract you have succeeded only in
accentuating the liabilities mentioned before,
much more than in the Ordinary Life Policy. But
what were your intentions in making these excessive overpayments? Presumably to buy paid-up
insurance. Did you actually get such insurance?
You did not; it is impossible to get it. *Your
Twenty-Payment Life policy is not paid-up in
twenty years, or at any other time.*

LIMITED PAYMENT POLICIES ARE NEVER PAID-UP

Let us look at the chart and see the actual costs
to your estate at a time when you are supposed to
be "paid-up." We enter the twenty-first year with
a cash value of $5,781.30 (in the policy), and no
more premiums to pay. Now what about this
cash—is it worthless? No one is ignorant of the
fact that money earns interest. We want to quote

again the words of Joseph B. Maclean:

> "It is evident that part of the cost where the
> the policy has a cash surrender value is repre-
> sented by interest on that value . . . The com-
> pany actually holds the amount of the cash
> value, and earns interest upon it which is not
> paid to the policy-holder. The insured there-
> fore pays over the interest on his cash value just
> as clearly as if he held the cash value himself,
> earned interest on it and paid the interest to the
> company."

There is no gainsaying Mr. Maclean's point.
The interest lost to your estate by leaving the cash
with the company is $346.88. This interest-loss
is a definite cost which must be included, and
would be included by a thorough accountant,
when auditing your estate. Rest assured that your
company, which is earning the interest, does appreciate the worth of your cash.

Under "Net Risk to Company," in the 21st year,
we find that the interest-contributed is securing
only $4,218.70 of net protection. You are paying
a rate of $82.22 per thousand—in the first year
of being "all paid-up." And at a time, if you con-
sult the Renewable Term column, when you
should only be paying $21.08 per thousand. In
your effort to avoid further payments, you have
succeeded only in sky-rocketing your costs. When
you are supposed to be fully paid-up, these costs
INCREASE from year to year.

We have previously pointed out that the size of the interest-factor is unimportant. We use six percent not because we believe everybody can get it, but because we want to avert confusion between interest paid on cash borrowed and interest contributed on cash still in the policy. In the present instance, if you think six percent too high, figure on any percent you can get. Whatever interest is being lost, then that amount represents your current expenditure for life insurance, after the policy is "paid-up." The important point to remember is that no Limited Payment policy can ever be "paid-up." The very name "Twenty-Payment Life" is a misnomer. The fact that you have made your twentieth payment means merely that your premium-payments cease. But when an agent, selling such a policy, maintains that premium-payments constitute your costs, when he intimates that the twentieth year brings your costs to an end, he is guilty of misrepresentation.

Now, what about the agent's promise that your savings is always yours for the asking? Suppose, in the twenty-third year, you want to borrow $2,000 of your cash value. The same shackles that make saving objectionable in any other policy hold true here. To get your cash, you are borrowing from your beneficiary who, at your death, will receive only $8,000. On that part of your cash value which you borrow, you pay $120 in interest; on the part remaining with the company, you con-

tribute interest.   To avail yourself of your savings
without restrictions, you would have to surrender
your policy and lose your protection.   It is true, in
an extremely narrow sense, that your savings are
available on demand.   But at what frightful cost!

In this chapter we have demonstrated the worth-
lessness of all Limited Payment plans.   How is it
possible that so inadvisable a type of insurance can
be sold with such ease?   The success of many advertising schemes depends not on the merit of the
product but upon the gullibility of the public.
Particularly where abstract mathematical calcula-
tions are necessary, the advertiser can rely upon
the limited knowledge of the prospective buyer.   A
clever sales-talk can usually victimize the best of us.

The Limited Payment policies could be sold
only to a buyer who has no knowledge of actuarial
principles.   The companies know this—and depend
upon it.   We shall let a representative company
be their spokesman.   In the *Confidential Handbook,* given to their most dependable agents, the
Travelers Insurance Company developes for their
agent the sales-talk to be employed in selling Limited Payment Policies.   As a man increases in age,
his remaining span of years grows less.   Therefore,
the company, wishing to get as much premium as
possible, attempts to crowd the payment into a
small number of years.   That is, the agent is in-
structed to sell to an old man, not Twenty-Payment Life, but Fifteen-Payment Life, or even

Ten-Payment Life. And of course, the payments being fewer, are considerably higher. But, lest there be one among us who sees the fallacies in the Limited Payment Plan, they caution their agent with these exact words:

> "Of course every form is worth what it costs, but the average man cannot be expected to make actuarial calculations for himself, or even to follow them, and it is only natural for him to become discouraged when his premium payments total more than the face of the contract. Under such circumstances it would be hard to get him to listen to any explanations, and he will tend to hold a grievance against insurance in general. A dissatisfied customer of this kind is not a good advertisement. This sort of dissatisfaction can be eliminated at the start by selling Limited Payment Policies at the higher ages. This is, of course, only a general rule which applies to the average man. When a man understands insurance and knows what he is getting so that the chance of disappointment is minimized, there is no reason why he should not buy Ordinary Life Insurance if he wants it."

A tip for agents: if the buyer cannot be victimized with any Limited-Payment Plan, be content with the smaller overcharges in Ordinary Life.

CHAPTER NINE

WHY ENDOWMENTS SHOULD BE AVOIDED

You should be impressed by now with the topsy-turvy character of life insurance as it is sold today. The more attractively a company presents a policy, the less desirable and more costly it is bound to be. You discovered that the companies discourage the sale of Renewable Term. This form, consisting of pure insurance, contains no investment feature. They prefer to sell you Ordinary Life, a policy that entails excess payments for investment. They are more eager to sell Limited Payment plans, and praise them to the skies to induce you to buy. The bigger the investment-feature in the policy, the less insurance in the policy—the more eloquent is the sales-talk. Hence, we are led to the remarkable conclusion that life insurance is an institution marked by a peculiar aversion to selling life insurance.

The type of contract that most rapidly ceases to be an insurance policy, that most swiftly becomes just an investment scheme, is the Endowment. This form has many variants; for our purpose it will be sufficient to consider the 20-Year Endowment—a perennial company favorite.

The 20-Year Endowment is a combination of a 20-Year Term contract and a pure endowment, which begin and end together. Tons of literature have been distributed by the companies, extolling the advantages resulting from this combination. By the time the policy matures, if you would believe the companies, the protection feature will have cost you nothing; moreover, you make a profit.

And an examination of the figures seems to sustain the companies. A $10,000 20-Year Endowment, taken out at age 35, requires a premium of $420.90. After twenty payments, when the policy matures, you will have paid in $8,418. Since the company at that time must pay you the face of the policy, $10,000, it can assure you that you have made a profit of $1,582. And you will have received insurance "absolutely free" for twenty years!

The companies, apparently, have a marvelous argument here. For if you had purchased a 20-Year Term by itself, at an average yearly premium of $100, it would terminate in twenty years, you would not get a cent back, and it would have cost you about $2,000. But by buying it wrapped up with a savings feature, you get the 20-Year Term contract free, and a bonus of $1,582 to boot.

Then what could Mr. W. F. Gephart, Dean of

the Financial School of Washington University, have meant by saying, "Life insurance is not an investing institution. It can never return to the buyer a profit"?

And why did Mr. Roger Babson advise you to ". . . buy life insurance as protection the same as you would buy automobile insurance, but think twice before buying it as an investment"?

Could these men have been unaware of the wonderful "advantages" of the 20-Year Endowment policy? Or were they keen enough to see through half-truths and misrepresentation?

What sharp practices are the companies guilty of now?

They conveniently forget to mention that the interest they have earned on your enormous over-payments has not only been sufficient to pay for the insurance, but has provided the meager "profit." This can readily be seen if you suppose that you had annually invested the amount of your premium, $420.90, over a 20-year period. Compounded at four percent, your investment at the end of the period would amount to more than thirteen thousand dollars. Consequently, it is absurd to believe that there is any way of getting something "free" in life insurance. What your principal doesn't pay for, your interest pays for. Furthermore, in the Endowment policy, both principal and interest are returned *only if you live*.

Let us look again at the component parts of the 20-Year Endowment—the Term and the pure endowment. The Term part is non-convertible and non-renewable; it is inexpensive but it has all the disadvantages of a short-term contract. The pure endowment part, considered by itself, is one of the most undesirable investment schemes ever devised. In fact, it is comparable more to a lottery than to an investment method. The participants in a pure endowment proposition each agree to pay at designated intervals a specified sum into a common fund. The payments continue, let us say, for twenty years. During that period, any members of the group who die get no return whatsoever: their payments are declared forfeit. At the expiration of the period, the surviving members draw out their respective shares of the accumulated fund. Since the venture, being in the nature of a gamble against death, involves a loss of money to your estate if you die, you would be quite imprudent to participate in it. On the other hand, the Term part does not recommend itself, since the Renewable forms possess all its merits with none of its faults.

Few people would want to buy either one of the parts of the 20-Year Endowment separately. Why, then, do so many fall for them in combination? For, when they are combined, the drawbacks of each are magnified. Let us remember that the 20-Year Endowment clings tenaciously to the name "insurance policy."   Insurance is bought as protection against death; under the two-faced Endowment contract, only one part of the contract holds if you die: the Term feature—protection. Every dollar of the huge "savings" in the policy is forfeited.   The companies never can claim that the protection afforded by the Endowment is any more than that in a 20-Year Term.   Yet, for the same amount of death benefit, you start out—at age 35—by paying four times as much for the 20-Year Endowment.   Or if you live to get a return from the pure endowment part of the contract, the protection element ceases to have meaning.

When the companies sell you two mutually exclusive items in one contract, they cannot supply both.   *For unless you accomplish the contradiction of both dying and living at the same time, you must lose one of the items you pay for: if you die, you lose your savings; if you survive, you lose your protection.*   In either case, the peculiarities of the contract compel you to sacrifice one feature.

Let us see how much you are paying for this privilege.   It is our supposition that, at age 35, you took out a $10,000 Non-Participating 20-Year Endowment.   Look carefully at the chart on the next page.

CURRENT-COST ANALYSIS OF 20-YEAR ENDOWMENT POLICY
(NON-PARTICIPATING—TAKEN OUT AT AGE 35)

Age	Year	Face Amount of Policy	Cash Value	Net Risk to Company or Actual Protection	Premium	Interest Contributed on Cash Value at 6%	Actual Cost for Net Risk	Extended Term Insurance Yrs	Extended Term Insurance Cash	Actual Cost per Thousand	1-Year Renewable Term Rates
35	1	$10,000 —	None	= $10,000.00	$420.90	+ None =	$420.90			$ 42.09	$ 8.82
39	5	10,000 —	$1,536.80	= 8,463.20	420.90	+ $92.21 =	513.11	15	$ 465.80	60.62	9.45
44	10	10,000 —	3,714.90	= 6,285.10	420.90	+ 222.89 =	643.79	10	4,291.90	102.42	11.19
49	15	10,000 —	6,641.00	= 3,359.00	420.90	+ 398.46 =	819.36	5	7,659.70	243.92	14.38
53	19	10,000 —	9,260.70	= 739.30	420.90	+ 555.64 =	976.54	1	9,577.30	1,320.89	18.38
54	20	10,000 —	10,000.00	= None	420.90						

[126]

What are the terrific costs you incur for your estate if you die within the 20-Year period. The first thing that strikes our eye as we analyze the chart, is that by the fifth year you have sufficiently overpaid for your protection to carry the face amount of the policy for the remaining fifteen years. In fact, your excess payments are more than sufficient. You will recall that in any reserve-bearing policy, if you lapse, the company will apply your overpayments toward "Extended Term Insurance." In this policy, the company cannot extend your insurance past the 20th year. Therefore, if you accept the extended term option at this time, any additional overpayment must be returned in cash when the policy terminates. As early as the fifth year there is an extra overpayment of $465.80; this sum would be returned to you, provided you take the option and live for the duration of the contract. It is evident, then, that by the fifth year you have more than fulfilled the cost requirements of the protection part of the policy. Since you have already paid for your $10,000 protection for the next fifteen years, and since any premiums paid in after the fifth year cannot increase your protection, it must be that these additional payments are your savings—the other part of your contract.

They are savings—in a narrow, limited sense of the word. In the same sense, however, we have heard the payments made into various lottery schemes described as "savings." It is possible to compare these premium-payments with true savings if you accept the option of extended insurance in the fifth year and annually invest the amount of your premiums elsewhere. Then, if you die, your beneficiary receives not only the $10,000 death benefit, the maximum within the policy, but your full savings and accumulated interest on them, as well. For no investing institution, other than life insurance, requires forfeiture of savings at death. Moreover, even if you survive the period, your accumulated savings and interest will return you more than you could have gained under the terms of the Endowment policy. Thus, in either case—whether you live or die—your estate would be in a better condition.

No clearer illustration than the Endowment contract can be summoned to prove the futility of mixing saving with protection. When an individual takes out a cash-value policy, he is agreeing to buy both insurance and investment. The "savings" element here shoots the combined costs up so high that he discovers he cannot continue paying for both; he would like to drop or postpone the investment part, and carry just the protection which is indispensable and which alone he can afford. But the terms of the policy demand that he pay for both—or carry neither. As we examine the costs in this policy, we will perceive why most holders of Endowments very shortly find themselves carrying neither.

The enormity of the liabilities you create for your estate in this policy can best be appreciated by referring again to the chart. In the fifteenth year (at age 49), we observe a cash value of $6,641 —which means that you are a 66 percent co-insurer of your own protection. In this policy, more than in any other type policy, you rapidly assume the risks and responsibilities of your insurance company. You are now in the insurance business more than your company is. The net risk to the company is only $3,359.

To calculate your costs for this net protection, add the "Interest contributed" to the premium. You will find your actual cost is $819.36 for $3,359 of protection. Your rate-per-thousand, therefore, amounts to $243.92. The rate for 1-Year Renewable Term at age 49 is $14.38.

In the nineteenth year, you have all but succeeded in pushing the company's risk out of your policy. Your cash value, your greatest liability, is now $9,260.70. You have reduced the company's risk to $739.30. Adding up your costs for this meager protection, you discover that you are paying the almost incredible rate of $1,320.89 *per thousand* at a time when it is purchasable for $18.38.

* * *

Advanced life insurance men rarely attempt to

defend the 20-Year Endowment—its deficiencies are too obvious. Their sole "defense," when they offer one, is that few people carry 20-Year Endowments, that compared to the total number of policies in force the number of Endowments extant is negligible. The Metropolitan, for example, supplies figures to show that only 3.7 percent of its policies are 20-Year Endowments.

Have we, then, justification to indict all life insurance because Endowments are bad? Assuredly, we have. The reason lies in the inclusive scope of Endowment-type policies. *For all policies except Term are Endowments.*

At the end of the chapter on dividends, we divided insurance contracts into two main categories: those in which you create co-insurance, and those in which you do not. The only policies in which no self-insurance is created are the various Term contracts.* In all other type policies, co-insurance is created; at the end of a specified period, this self-insurance (consisting of your excess payments) becomes equal to the face amount of the contract: the policy then endows.

The 20-Year Endowment endows after twenty premium payments; taken out at age 35, it would endow at age 55. It is, therefore, identical to an Endowment at Fifty-Five. If you were to thumb

---

*A special case is the Term Expectancy contract. Although a small cash value is created in it, it is a Term form, since it does not endow.

through a rate book, you would find dozens of similar policies.

You would discover Endowments at Sixty, at Sixty-Five, at Eighty, at Eighty-Five, and so forth. You would, moreover, discover a wide variety of Endowments at Age Ninety-Six. But you would look in vain to find them under that name. They are labelled Ordinary Life, Straight Life, 20-Payment Life, 30-Payment Life, and the like. *But they are all Endowments*.

The above policies are similar in that they all create self-insurance: they differ only in the length of time required for them to endow. The shorter the endowing period, the greater will be each payment. This is necessarily so because the cash value, which will ultimately equal the face amount of the contract if the insured lives, must be composed of a smaller number of excess payments. That is why the 10-Year Endowment requires a larger premium than the 20-Year Endowment.

We are ready to draw important conclusions. The 20-Year Endowment policy is, by any standard of judgment, objectionable. The 30-Year Endowment must likewise be objectionable: the difference between the two is merely one of degree. A 62-Year Endowment, which is tantamount to an Ordinary Life or a Limited Payment Life taken out at age 35, is open to the same objections. The mere fact that the payments are stretched over sixty-two years is no extenuation. While it is true that you can lose money faster in a 20-Year Endowment, we cannot see how this exonerates Ordinary Life.

The question that confronts every policy-holder —What policy shall I carry?—ultimately becomes a choice between an endowment policy and an insurance policy. It cannot be answered without reference to the intentions of the insured. Are your needs best answered by a policy which contains a minimum of insurance and a maximum of "investment"? Or are you primarily interested in protecting your family?

In any case, if you understand the opposing functions of the two types of policies, if you are aware of the dangers to each function that come from mixing them in one policy, we have fulfilled the main part of our task. In our opinion, once the policy-holder comprehends the nature of his problem, he is capable of independent judgment. Primarily because of a lack of this understanding, the average policy-holder today is carrying policies that will frustrate the purposes for which he bought them. The anti-social attitude of the insurance companies can be met and defeated only by a growing awareness on the part of the policy-holders.

In our next chapter, we will deal with the companies' ace-in-the-hole—the "net cost" presentation. The deceptiveness of this high-pressure sales argument has blinded millions of policy-holders to the inadequacy of their present contracts. Despite its patent fallaciousness, it remains the most effective armament the companies can muster to deter policy-holders from purchasing pure insurance, to persuade them to buy high-priced policies, and to discourage them from rewriting or twisting.

CHAPTER TEN

THE NET-COST FABLE: HOW AGENTS JUGGLE FIGURES

A young mathematical genius walked into our office the other day with a dazzling scheme. He had devised a plan, he told us, whereby we could keep ourselves supplied with shoes for twenty years, averaging one pair a year, and the entire supply wouldn't cost us a penny.

We gasped. Could he be serious? "It's impossible," we decided. "It costs money to manufacture shoes, the shoe-workers must be paid, the middle-man must make a profit . . . there is no honest way of getting shoes without paying for them."

The genius laughed. "My scheme is really very simple," he said; "it can be employed by anyone. Here it is. Go to Mr. A———, the shoe merchant, and deposit $30 with him. Repeat this transaction once a year for nineteen more years, each time taking a $10 pair of shoes. At the end of that time, you will have deposited with Mr. A———, a total of $600, and have received twenty pairs of shoes. With the passing of the 20th year, the merchant will be glad to pay you back $600.

"You will have gotten shoes absolutely free for twenty years. It will be an obvious bargain for you, and what is even more surprising, the merchant will be enthusiastic about it too. He will tell you to do it again, and to send your friends to get their shoes for nothing also."

We were skeptical. "If it's true," we said, "it's the most amazing thing we have ever heard. Because if it can be done with shoes, why can't we buy everything else for nothing? Don't you realize that if your scheme is workable, you have abolished the cost of living?"

"That's exactly what I've done," said the Young Man proudly. "As a matter of fact, I ought to confess that it's not really my idea. I got the idea from the way life insurance is sold. Insurance, you know, is a commodity, the price of which can be easily determined—more easily, in fact, than the price of shoes. And once you know the price of an article, it is child's play to reduce that price to zero. . . .

"An agent once tried to sell me a 20-Payment Life policy. He showed me how, over twenty years, my protection would cost me nothing. So, being a mathematical genius, I saw that protection isn't the only thing that can be sold that way. I explained the proposition to Mr. A——, and now I'm his agent, selling shoes for him on a commission basis. I can show his customers that they can get shoes from him for nothing. What is more, I can show you how you can buy any article under the sun in the same costless manner."

We were very much impressed. We had visions of living cost-free, of indulging in every whim and luxury. But our common sense rebelled; it was too perfect a scheme to work. "What," we inquired, "is the catch?"

"There is no catch," he said. "Every year that you pay the shoe-merchant $30, you are, of course, paying him $20 over and above the price of the shoes. He invests this difference of $20 every year. At compound interest, he will have no trouble in returning all the money you paid him, and will have enough surplus (from the interest) to pay himself the full cost of twenty pairs of shoes. What the shoe-merchant will do is this: he will not only be selling you shoes, he will also be acting as your banker; and he will realize profit from both ventures.

"It will be a simple thing for him to get 4% or more on your money; the interest compounded over twenty years will more than pay for your shoes."

For a moment we pondered. "Is the shoe-merchant permitted by law to be a banker?"

"Well, the law isn't very clear on it," the Young Man replied. "By mixing shoe-selling with his banking business, the merchant can so confuse the legislature and State Banking Department that they won't apply banking laws to him. In the same manner, the life insurance companies confuse the law-makers by mixing protection with banking—no banking obligations apply to *them*. And if the insurance companies can get by with it, why can't any other form of business?"

"Suppose we die before the twenty years are up," we asked; "will we get back the amount of our overpayments?"

"Of course not," he said in surprise. "You don't get back your savings in an insurance policy if you die—why expect to get them back here?"

Such forfeiture seemed strange to us, but the Young Man assured us that policy-holders forfeit savings every day, which must make it all right. "It's a precedent," he said.

"We don't think we want to buy shoes your way," we decided finally. "If the shoe-merchant's plan means forfeiture of our excess deposits if we die, then why can't we just buy shoes and save the difference somewhere else, where it cannot be lost? By doing it that way, the interest would still pay for the shoes, and the savings would be ours under all circumstances."

"Nobody ever said that you couldn't save elsewhere," he admitted cheerfully. "Any man who wants to, and can afford it, can save or invest money and use the interest to pay for whatever he wants. But sixty-five million holders of insurance policies rely upon insurance companies to do their investing for them.   In their purchase of insurance, they eagerly grasp the opportunity to lose their savings at death; hence, it is not unlikely that they would be equally delighted to have the same opportunity in their other purchases."

"It seems impossible to us," we declared, "that people are willing to take the chance of losing their savings in the event of death."

"They are willing," the genius volunteered, "because they don't know any better.   And this is why they all fall for the scheme; the insurance companies have blinded them with the 'Net Cost Fairy Tale.' "

We were puzzled.

The Young Man went on to explain.   "By just considering the *net* payments, and disregarding the interest, the companies can show that, *after a given number of years,* the insured can get back all his *net* payments.   They allow the 'savings fund' to work for them: they get the interest.   The larger the overpayments, of course, the greater will be the amount of interest earned.   Consequently, the more you overpay for insurance, the less will be your *net cost*.   BUT THE GREATER WILL BE YOUR GROSS COST."   (Premiums plus the interest you contribute on savings held by the company.)

We began to see light.   The Young Man drew up the following table, showing net cost for a $10,-000 Whole Life policy at age 35.

```
Net premiums for 20 years  (20 times $200.60) . . . . . $4,012.00
Cash surrender value at the end of 20th year . . . . . $3,107.50
                                                       ──────────
Net cost for 20 years  (by subtraction) . . . . . . . . . . . . $  904.50
Net cost for 1 year . . . . . . . . . . . . . . . . . . . . . . . . . . . . . . . . $   45.23
           Net cost per $1,000 = $4.52
```

"This is a conventional net-cost chart," the Young Man explained. "The insurance companies would have you believe that it is a genuine analysis of costs. It is not; it is a snare for unwary policy-holders. At the end of the 20th year, you can sit down with a pencil and paper and subtract the amount of the cash value ($3,107.50) from the net amount of your premiums as often as you like; you will always find that your net cost is $45.23. Attempt, however, to pay for your insurance by sending the company a check for $45.23 instead of $200.60 and you will appreciate the false theoretical character of the whole net-cost analysis.

"No matter how often you make the subtraction on paper, it will continue to remain without meaning. You are merely juggling figures. You are subtracting the cash value—*when it is held within the policy, not in your possession*. Unless you actually surrender your insurance and sacrifice your protection, you cannot get your cash unencumbered. And until the cash is in your possession, there is no possible way of calculating net cost. For, if you die while the contract is in force, the *net* cost to your estate is the *total amount of premiums paid*. The company, ignoring its entire net-cost theory, requires you to forfeit your over-payments.

"During your life, as at death, the company presentation of net-cost never has anything to do with what you are actually paying. One way of computing costs is to regard your constant, large premium as securing a steadily decreasing amount of net insurance (decreased by the amount of your own money, the cash value, in the policy). You are also contributing to the company the interest-worth of your cash—a cost which must be added to the premium. This *gross cost* (premium plus interest contributed) which is buying the amount of net protection in the policy, is high, and will get higher every year that you keep the policy . . .

"And," continued the Young Man, "as we look at a $10,000 20-Payment Life net-cost chart, you can readily see that as your overpayments are larger, your net-cost will seem less. The sales-talk for this contract is a masterpiece. The company not only 'proves' that after twenty years the insurance will cost you nothing, but also that by the fifteenth year you begin to make a 'profit'. The cash value in the 15th year is $3,840.20. After making a premium payment of $278.20, your cash value will be increased by $337.70 over the preceding year. Deduct your premium from that increase; your 'profit' is $59.50."

"Then if the insurance in the 15th year is costing us nothing," we asked, "why can't we stop paying premiums, and have the company mail us a check for the difference ($59.50), or our profit?"

This disgusted him. "Haven't you ever heard of 'paper profit'?"

We yielded the point.

"After twenty years," he went on, "your protection has apparently cost you nothing; you have even made a 'profit' of $97.50. The net-cost is still a fairy tale, the 'profit' is still imprisoned within your policy. If you die you lose both 'profit' and principal; if you live, you can retrieve them only by giving up your insurance."

As the Young Man showed us the net-cost under the Endowment plans, he laughed satanically. "This is a gem," he said. "So enormous are the overpayments here that they seem not only to eliminate all costs for protection, but in time to accumulate the full amount of the protection—and make a sizable profit. If you are fortunate enough to live the full period, you get back the entire $10,000. The real beauty of the Endowment lies in the fact that you are buying protection against death, yet must live to get back your overpayments. By means of net-cost, the companies can sell two mutually exclusive items in one contract: in order to get both, you would have to live and die at the same time. Despite the advantages to be gained by living throughout the Endowment period, innumerable people have been foolish enough to die and consequently lose their savings."

Here the Young Man grew wistful. "If I only had enough capital," he sighed longingly, "to start an insurance company . . ."

"Cheer up," we advised him; "maybe you can duplicate the success of the insurance companies by applying their practices to the shoe business."

"It cannot be done in shoes," the genius admitted. "Sometimes I think that the insurance companies, through long years of propaganda, have monopolized the gullibility of the public. Everybody sees through the fallacy when I try to apply net-cost to selling shoes."

The Young Man left.

* * *

So never again let an agent palm off on you the "Net-Cost Fairy Tale." Whenever he mentions "net cost," be on your guard lest he misrepresent the policy and try to conceal its true cost. The agent, with a fat commission in view, may ignore the interest-worth of your money and the hypothetical nature of your cash value. Thousands of policy-holders have been dissuaded from buying inexpensive policies—such as 20-Year Renewable Term, which, at age 35, costs about half as much as Ordinary Life—because Ordinary Life has a lower "net cost." Other policy-holders have bought Limited Payment Life policies in preference to Ordinary Life, because of the deceptive net-cost comparison. Still others, deluded by the hope of big "profits" in the Endowment contract, have permitted net-cost to blind them to the viciousness of Endowments; due to their agent's cleverness in presenting net-cost, they have purchased contracts that contain a minimum of protection for a maximum of outlay. Always remember that the more you pay for insurance, the less net protection you get, or the greater will be the loss of money to your estate if you die.

Moral: The Lower the Net Cost, the Greater Your Overpayments and Actual Cost.

CHAPTER ELEVEN

INDUSTRIAL INSURANCE: A SNARE FOR WORKERS

American workers are bitterly aware of their need for life insurance. For them, the menace of insecurity, the threat of sudden death attended by pauper burial and unprotected dependents, is formidable and ever-present. So it is a holiday task for the largest and most efficient high-pressure selling organizations in the world to induce them to carry Industrial insurance—on the "easy-payment" plan. This form of insurance provides a few hundred dollars in the event of death and calls for a weekly outlay of five cents or a small multiple of that amount, such as a dime, fifteen cents, or a quarter. Hence, it is commonly known as "Five-and-Dime" insurance.

Another current term for this kind of protection is "Burial" insurance. Fifteen million workers or their children can theoretically have funerals costing an aggregate sum of seventeen *billion* dollars— the total face amount of the insurance in force. Burial insurance? In one year, the nickels and dimes which the working class "buries" in the insurance companies amount to eight hundred million dollars. The average worker, that is to say, expends about six percent of his annual income for the single item of Industrial insurance.

The vastness of the business has made it respectable, exempting it from the general condemnation that smaller rackets evoke. Nevertheless, investigators of Industrial insurance have arisen to protest against its iniquities. Comprehensive indictments have been drawn up by Dr. Maurice Taylor, Percy E. Budlong, Jack Bradon, L. Seth Schnitman, Abraham Epstein, and others. Nor does one have to be an expert to discover the defectiveness of Industrial insurance. The discovery weighs heavily upon the consciences of most of the men who sell it. When Abraham Epstein published an article entitled "The Insurance Racket," in the American Mercury (September, 1930), many Industrial agents wrote to him, bewailing and apologizing for their calling. Here are excerpts from two typical letters:

> "As an Industrial agent I feel you merit the thanks of the thousands of Industrial insurance agents who are daily driven and hounded to sell this petty larceny form of insurance. We agents sell this stuff, but we hate to do it; we know that the companies are robbing the industrial classes with a contract which is scandalously exorbitant in rate and negligible in benefits."

> "I had agents come to my home and tell me

with tears in their eyes that they hate this Industrial insurance robbery but they cannot help
it. Their wives and children must eat."

Industrial insurance is big-business, levying an
enormous tribute upon those least able to pay.
Masquerading as a benevolent institution devoted
to the protection of widows and orphans, it has
prospered at the expense of its ostensible beneficiaries. Some indication of what this expense
has been may be gleaned from its phenomenal size
and growth. In 1910, Industrial insurance cost the
working class 103 million dollars; in 1920, $257
million; in five years the expenditure jumped to
half a billion; by 1930, it reached 803 million and
has been able to hold its own against the storms
of the past five years. Here is aggrandizement
with a vengeance: Industrial insurance is a business that, barring economic calamity, doubles itself as a matter of course every few years. The
familiar law of concentration has not spared Industrial insurance. Of the sixty-five companies
reporting to the Insurance Year Book, the "Big
Three"—The Metropolitan, The Prudential, and
The John Hancock—account for almost nine-
tenths of the business.

On the face of it, Industrial insurance is healthy
enough and big enough to protect the working
class against certain hazards. Yet it has failed—
miserably. Back in 1906, Louis D. Brandeis, now
a Supreme Court Justice, dubbed Industrial insur-

ance "The greatest life-insurance wrong." Let us examine the business as it is today, to determine, on the basis of accomplishment, whether there is any foundation to the wide-spread belief that the wrong has been righted.

The best way to begin is to look at a policy. One's suspicions are aroused immediately by the abstruseness of the terminology employed. The opening paragraph of a Metropolitan contract will illustrate:

> "IN CONSIDERATION of the payment of the premium stated in the schedule on page 4 hereof, on or before each Monday doth hereby agree subject to the conditions below and on page 2 hereof each of which is hereby made a part of this contract and contracted by every person entitled to claim hereunder to be a part hereof to pay as an endowment 20 years from the date hereof if the insured be then living, upon surrender of this policy and evidence of premium payment hereunder, the amount stipulated in said schedule."

Well, skip it. The point to be observed is that this is part of a contract, to be read and signed by two parties, henceforth binding them to certain conditions; the company deliberately making the contract so unintelligible to the buyer that he will know nothing of what he is getting. The reasons behind the obfuscation become apparent when we consider the disadvantageous terms and provisions which he unwittingly accepts.

The most inexcusable of these provisions is the so-called Express Warranty or "Sound Health" clause. Stripped of verbiage, it declares that if the policy-holder is not in "sound health" on the date the policy is issued, or if he has ever had any one of a long list of diseases, the policy is void; in that case, the company need not pay a death claim, its liability being limited to returning the premiums paid on the policy. Most Industrial policy-holders never heard of the clause; those who have do not understand that its effect is to destroy the certainty of protection, since any one of the diseases may be present in a latent form without the knowledge of the "insured." Every physician knows that the victims of such diseases are usually not aware of their existence until the advanced stages set in; moreover, few people who reach middle-age escape the incipient stage of at least one of the catalog of ailments listed in Express Warranty.

The Supreme Court of Nebraska comments (49 Nebr. 842):

> "What sane man would consciously warrant that ever since his childhood he had not had any disease of the heart, liver, lungs, kidneys, bladder, stomach, or bowels? No sane man would consciously consent that on the literal truth of his negative answer . . . should depend the validity of a life-insurance policy."

In 282 Southwestern Reporter, 633, it is held:

> "It would seem unjust to void a policy based upon statements made in good faith by proving after death by expert medical examiners that in their opinion death was caused by some latent ailment of which the insured . . . knew nothing and had no means of knowing, in the absence of a medical examination."

The company does more than protect itself against fraud on the part of the applicant: through the Express Warranty provision, it protects itself against his lack of omniscience. Percy E. Budlong, Official Reporter, United States Senate, points out the injustice of the clause:

> "No one will claim that educated and experienced business men could be sold an ordinary life policy containing a binding condition precedent of absolute freedom from disease. No ship-owner would specifically warrant his vessel free from all concealed defects in hull or machinery . . . No owner of a building would warrant that there was no fire risk about his premises. Then why make the poor, ignorant Industrial applicant warrant that he is and always has been perfectly healthy?"

That the provision tends to defeat the purpose of insurance is attested by the innumerable court cases on record. Case after case concerns beneficiaries who, suing to collect the death benefit promised in the policy, were successfully denied any compensation on the ground that, at the issue-date of the contract, the "insured" had a latent disease which subsequently proved fatal. There are even cases in which the policy was voided because of an incipient disease which contributed nothing to the death of the policy-holder. In the instance of Barker v. Metropolitan Life (188 Mass. 543), after the company physician had declared the insured to be in sound health, it later appeared that he had cystic disease of the kidneys. The insured ultimately died—of pneumonia. The company repudiated the findings of its own doctor, but failed to show any connection between the pneumonia and the alleged kidney disease. In its refusal to allow a death benefit, it was, nevertheless, sustained by the courts. Another case: a policy-holder who apparently had hernia when he bought the policy, succumbed to valvular heart disease and dropsy (184 Indiana, 722). The court held that inasmuch as the policy was voided by the existence of hernia, the actual causes of death could have no influence upon such a policy.

On the basis of the "Sound Health" clause alone, it can be seen that an Industrial policy is a gamble. Not until after the death of the insured can the beneficiary know whether the contract was ever in force. If the company contests the policy, the beneficiary—notwithstanding his hypothetical equality before the law—is compelled to accept whatever terms of settlement the company deigns to offer. For the class served by Industrial insurance cannot afford the expense and delay of litigation; the company, on the other hand, is prepared to use the best legal talent available, and to appeal and re-appeal if the verdict should be adverse.

Policy-holders overlook the intent of Express Warranty not only because it is obscurely worded but because another provision apparently nullifies it. This provision—and agents are always quick to point it out to the prospective buyer—is the Incontestability clause. Unlike the rest of the contract, it is distinguished for its lucidity, since it is a selling-point. Its main portion reads:

> "After this policy shall have been in force, during the lifetime of the Insured, for one full year from its date, it shall be incontestable, except for non-payment of premium."

The clause is nicely worded and should sound very good with music. It should especially hearten those who have been denied a death benefit by virtue of the Express Warranty provision. How, it may be asked, can the two clauses be reconciled? The joker is contained in the words *shall have been in force*. Although the insured pays premiums for a number of years, that fact alone does not signify that the policy was ever in force. The company is contractually justified in its contention that, if the "Sound Health" clause was violated, the policy has been void from the beginning. It is tricky but true that a policy which has never been *in force* can never be incontestable. This delightful technicality, it should be mentioned, has so offended the sense of fitness of several judges when it has been raised in court, that the companies were subjected to blistering censure. Consequently as far as the courts are concerned, the argument is falling into disuse; the companies still employ it, however, in the unrecorded thousands of cases that never come to court.

Another questionable provision in the contract, one which has been the source of considerable dispute and disappointment, is the "Facility-of-Payment" clause. In substance it provides that:

> "The company may make any payment provided herein to the insured, or to any relative by blood or connection by marriage of the insured, or to any other person appearing to the company to be equitably entitled to such payment by reason of having incurred expense on behalf of the insured, or for his or her burial; and the production of a receipt signed by any of said persons shall be conclusive evidence that all claims under this policy have been satisfied."

In other words, the company can legally discharge all its obligations by paying any relative of the policy-holder or a virtual stranger, such as an undertaker. What is more, if the company can find someone who is willing to accept less than the amount called for, and can persuade him to sign a receipt, it is absolved from any further payment. The average policy-holder believes that the beneficiary he selected at the time he signed his application will receive the proceeds of his policy when it matures as a death claim. While they encourage him in this belief, it is not warranted: at his death, the company has the contractual right to ignore his intended beneficiary.

The companies defend this right on the ground that it "facilitates" settlement of the claim. Admitting the element of truth in their contention, it is still obvious that the clause is open to the grossest of abuse. Citation of a few court cases will illustrate how it can thwart the express wishes of the policy-holder. In the case of Brennan v. Prudential Insurance Company (32 Atlantic Reporter 1042), the sentiment of the Court of Common Pleas of Lackawanna County, Pa., is of interest:

> "Here the company paid but a part of the money [less than half], and set up this to bar the whole. This, it is contended, does not fall within the strict terms of the policy, because it is only the payment of the amount named in the policy, and the production of a receipt for that full amount, that is to work satisfaction. To allow of anything less than this, it is argued, is to invite fraud. If the company may select their own party, and settle with him on his own terms, they can pick up anybody, and discharge themselves with a mere song."

The case moved on to the trial court which, though granting the reasonableness of the foregoing argument, was compelled nonetheless to

sustain the company.   Commenting upon the inclusive powers which the Facility-of-Payment
clause confers upon the company, the trial justice
said:

> "If, therefore, the company may determine to
> whom they will pay, they may also make their
> own terms with him; and if he sees fit to take 50
> cents on the dollar, or any other sum, in settle-
> ment of the amount insured, it concerns no one
> but himself, and the company are discharged."

In the case of Diggs v. Metropolitan Life (vol.
70, Pittsburgh Legal Journal, p. 983), the syllabus
informs us that:

> "Plaintiff, brother and beneficiary of [the de-
> ceased policy-holder] sued to recover on a policy
> which contained the 'facility of payment' clause.
> . . . The evidence showed that the brother, . . .
> who was beneficiary in the policy, acting upon
> his supposed right to the money, had incurred
> the expense of burying the insured, and the hus-
> band, who received the money from the com-
> pany, paid no part of these expenses."

Adhering to the letter of the contract, the Common Pleas Court of Allegheny County upheld the
company, but remarked:

> "We do not understand why people buy and pay
> for insurance of this kind.   It is no doubt true
> that the clause in question would sometimes pre-
> vent expense [and litigation], but it certainly
> puts in the hands of the agents of companies car-

rying on this sort of insurance a power which is very likely to be abused, especially if it be allowed that a payment of less than the whole sum is sufficient to discharge the company, as the agent will be *likely to pay the party who is willing to take the least money. We cannot help but believe that a great injustice has been done ... but we do not see how it can be remedied, in view of the terms of the policy.* (Our emphasis.)"

The two provisions already examined—Express Warranty and Facility-of-Payment—in themselves establish the vicious one-sidedness of the Industrial contract. Indeed, the very right of an Industrial policy to be called a contract is open to question. Its deficiencies show up glaringly if we compare it with an ordinary life-insurance policy which is designed, not for the working class, but for the middle and upper classes. First of all, the ordinary policy contains neither of the objectionable clauses: the policy is incontestable after one or two years with no strings attached; and the death benefit is promptly paid to the beneficiary previously chosen by the insured.

An ordinary policy, moreover, is assignable; that is, it can be used as security for an outside loan; the policy-holder simply designates the lender as the person to whom he wants the death claim paid. An Industrial policy is not assignable; its holder cannot offer it as security for a loan and no lender would accept it if he did, since neither the insured nor the creditor knows who will receive the death

payment. This provision, known as "Invalidity
of Assignment", destroys much of the usefulness
of the policy during the life of the insured.

The ordinary policy, after its third year, grants
a loan privilege to the policy-holder; he may
borrow as much cash as the policy contains, leaving the protection in force. Industrials have no
loan value at any time; the only way a policy-
holder can retrieve any of his cash is to carry the
policy for a full ten years, after which he may surrender it for a small part of what he has paid in
and cancel the insurance. In this connection, it
is worth mentioning that most Industrials taken
out do not survive the first year.

So much for the comparison of provisions. Dis-
criminating against the Industrial policy-holder at
every turn, the company, as Jack Bradon has
stated, "assumes the right to dictate the rights and
obligations of both parties to the contract, and the
insured is bound by the discretion of the other
party to the contract."

Industrial insurance, even if we forget for the
moment its outrageously inequitable features,
must be condemned for its excessively high cost.
Ordinary insurance costs far more than it should;
a comparative premium analysis discloses that Industrial insurance costs about 33 percent more
than ordinary. In fact, the usual comparison is
made on the basis of "net cost"—computed by
adding the premiums for ten years and deducting

the cash surrender value available in the policy at the end of that time. While for technical reasons we do not approve of the net-cost analysis, it is admissible in the present instance. The comparison is startling: *The holder of an Industrial whole-life policy has a net-cost eight times higher than that of the holder of an ordinary whole-life policy.* In the wonderland of life insurance, the most extortionate type of protection is reserved for the poorest people.

As a partial extenuation of the Industrial rates, it may be said that the inefficient weekly method of collecting premiums entails a greater overhead expense. Assuming the validity of the argument, the fact remains that the blame rests not with the Industrial policy-holders but rather with the companies. They have learned that the largest profits come from the existing set-up; nothing, therefore, could induce them to abandon it. The continuance of the business depends upon the well-trained army of sharp, smooth-talking agents who, actuated by the slogan Keep Up Production, use every means to foist more and more policies on a market already oversold.

In view of the high-pressure way Industrial insurance is peddled, in view of its exorbitant cost, it is not surprising that an overwhelming percentage of policies is dropped, or lapsed, shortly after purchase. President Ecker of The Metropolitan Life has testified that 85 percent of the lapses occur

in the first year.   Eventual lapse or surrender is
the inevitable destiny of nineteen out of every
twenty policies sold.   The direct loss sustained by
the working class due to policies which were lapsed
during the five-year period 1928-32, has been con-
servatively estimated at 200 million dollars, and is
undoubtedly much greater.

The number of policies terminated for all
reasons during 1934 totalled 20 million, aggregat-
ing $4,400,000,000 of insurance.   Lapse or sur-
render, involving a complete or virtual loss to
policy-holders, accounted for 4.1 billion, or 93 percent of the total terminations.   In order to curb
the use of astronomical figures, we will take the
illustration suggested by Dr. Maurice Taylor. Out
of every thousand dollars taken off the books of
the insurance companies during 1934, lapse and
surrender exacted a toll of $930.

We are now approaching the crucial test of any
system of insurance.   The only valid reason for the
existence of life-insurance is that it presumably insures against the financial loss occasioned by
death; the payment of death benefits is its sole
object, and unless it efficiently fulfills that object,
it fails as a protection device.   What percent of
every thousand dollars taken off the books in 1934
went to pay death benefits?   The answer, according to the most reliable statistics, is *three* percent!
In 1934, when billions of dollars were completely
lost through lapse, when an additional billion

went for surrender, the companies actually paid death claims amounting to only 153 million dollars. The exact figures, taken from the Insurance Year Book (for the year ending December 31, 1934), pp. 412-413, are as follows:

Total Terminations $4,428,062,908
Terminations by Lapse........... 3,127,573,734
Terminations by Surrender....... 983,691,019
Terminations by Death.......... 153,570,202
  Note also:
Salaries and Commissions........$ 149,456,286

The failure of Industrial insurance to insure could not be more absolute.

What can be done about Industrial Insurance? Those who expect us to propose reforms will be disappointed. The question is not one of lowering rates or of liberalizing policy provisions. We can suggest, of course, that Industrial policyholders who have the means, buy ordinary insurance and drop their present Industrial policies, accepting, wherever possible, one of the "non-forfeiture" options. Others will be wise to discontinue their Industrial insurance in favor of the policies issued by the International Workers Order, a fraternal organization administered by the working class and offering death- and sick-benefits for remarkably low rates.

Merely to state the possible remedies, however, is to demonstrate their inadequacy. The simple and obvious truth is that the American working class cannot afford to pay for any insurance. We believe it is not essential here to dwell upon the statistics relating to the meagre annual income of the average worker. Only in the light of his insufficiency of income, it must be emphasized, does the viciousness of Industrial insurance become truly exposed. Billions of dollars that might have been spent for the necessaries of life, for milk and bread, have run to waste for flimsy insurance. In the impoverishment of the working class, the Industrial-insurance companies have done their part.

There is but one practical and humane program. The Federal Government must be forced to assume the responsibility of insuring the working class. That responsibility should not be confined to the payment of death benefits—just as the insecurity of workers is not limited to the hazard of sudden death. The program must include a well-rounded, comprehensive system of social insurance, no expense of which should be borne by the workers. Inasmuch as all the so-called contributory schemes of social insurance, such as the Wagner-Lewis "Social Security" Bill, must ultimately be paid for by those least able to bear the cost, they can be regarded as little more than a bookkeeping trick. Only a form of social insurance maintained by the taxation of the upper-income groups can afford the working class the security it needs. Workers can win such insurance

—perhaps including "burial insurance"—by "burying" their representatives in Congress under an avalanche of demands for the one adequate measure—The Workers' Unemployment, Old Age, and Social Insurance Act, known all over the country as the Frazier-Lundeen Bill.

CHAPTER TWELVE

LIFE INSURANCE AGENTS: PLANNERS— OR PEDDLERS?

You have read proof that in your insurance dealings you have been grossly victimized, that the gold you bought has turned out to be brass, that you have been taken in like a country bumpkin.

What are you going to do now? In our experience, no sooner than a man is shown how he has been deceived, his first impulse is to rush to his agent. In a mad effort to get his money's worth, he turns to the very source of his predicament. The same agent whose ignorance or greed made a mess of his insurance estate is to get the chance to begin all over again!

"A burnt child dreads the fire." But who are these agents, who—unlike fire—may burn you again and again without losing their lure? Are they men capable of determining your needs? Are they conscious of the fact that insurance is only one of the problems involved in planning an estate? Are they aware that as a man grows older he can secure adequate protection with less and less insurance?

How can they be? In many states, all that is necessary to become an agent is a desire to share in the quarter-of-a-billion-dollar commission toll exacted every year. If a man can read English, if he can calculate that the commission for a $10,000 Renewable Term policy is $26.50 while for a $10,000 20-payment Life it is $190.90, and can guide you accordingly, he is the stuff from which agents are made. Armed with *these* fundamental principles of insurance, he is prepared to lead you to security, to serve your each and every insurance need, to plan your estate—and to make as much money out of you as possible.

In other states, the companies are even more exacting; they insist on certain standards. Before the ordinary incompetent can become an agent he must first be thoroughly indoctrinated with the company's point of view. This is to guard against the possibility that he might serve the buyer to the disadvantage of the company.

In Pennsylvania, for example, the applicant must memorize a list of some ninety questions and answers. That is, the company which is accepting him as a prospective agent gives him this list with its answers. He memorizes these answers. The examination questions will be taken from this list and all that is expected of him is to repeat parrotwise the answers he memorized.

The following are specimen questions and answers given to an applicant by an insurance company. Remember, the answers are the company's —to be memorized by the applicant.

Q.: "How can a policy-holder lawfully be advised to drop an existing policy in one company to take out a new policy in another company?"

A.: "Cannot be done."

Q.: "Is it lawful for an Agent of one Company to satisfy a disgruntled policy-holder of another company."

A.: "Yes."

(These two questions are obviously contradictory. Just how "disgruntled" the insured must be before the agent can "satisfy" him is not stated; how much satisfaction the insured can get while keeping his existing liabilities and overcharges is perhaps explained in the next question.)

Q.: "What service can be given to a policy-holder to prevent him from becoming dissatisfied?   (a) by the Agent?"

A.: (a) "Explain all benefits and non-forfeiture values of policy. Make him understand the type of coverage carried and what it will do for him."

(In other words, the agent is to give the policy-holder the old standbys—the "Net Cost Fairy Tale," the dividend myth, the beauty of his "theoretical" cash value, etc.)

Q.: "What service (b) by the Company?"

A.: "Educational literature and seeing that Agents make service calls."

(The company may not distinguish between "educational literature" and propaganda.)

Q.: "What service (c) by the competitive agents?"

A.: By pointing out advantages of present policy
and refraining from attempts at twisting."
(Competitive Agents are warned to resist
temptation. "There must be honor among
thieves.")

Q.: "What obligation has the agent (a) to the
insured? (b) to the company? (c) to other
agents?"

A.: " (a) To render service. (b) Carry out its
instructions and wishes. (c) Apply the
Golden Rule."
(Get it? The insured is to get "service"
—that is, anything left after the company
has *its* "instructions and wishes" carried
out.)

Q.: "Of what value, if any, is an examination
[such as this] to secure a license (a) to the
agent? (b) to the public? (c) to the company?"

A.: " (a) Preparation for examination is educational. (b) Agents who are licensed as result from examination are well informed
and qualified to prescribe for insurance
needs of applicants. (*sic*) (c) Secures more
competent agents by weeding out poor or
unsuitable ones.
(Of what value, if any—?)

The required answers to the above questions clearly indicate that if an applicant understands insurance principles and answers honestly, he will be eliminated immediately.

But assume that the applicant has the guile of a ten-year-old child, and hence passes the examination. He will still know less about the workings of life insurance than a radio salesman understands the mechanism of his radio sets. The radio salesman knows that a certain set is a super-heterodyne; it is plainly stated on the box. You really get a break with the radio; if the salesman claims it has six tubes, you can look in the cabinet and see.

The insurance agent also knows the name of what he is selling you; if the policy is a 20-Payment Life, or a 10-Year Endowment, the fact is mentioned on the face of the contract. So far so good. Then the agent assures you that the 20-Payment Life is paid-up in 20 years. But, while you would insist on looking inside the radio, while you would demand and receive a demonstration before buying even a vacuum cleaner, you are content to take the agent's ballyhoo as gospel, to buy your insurance blindfold.

Can you deny that you bought your insurance in this unbusinesslike manner? Who was your agent? For whose benefit did you make the purchase? Were you thinking of your dependents,— or did you do it just to accommodate a brother-in-law or a friend?

We are reminded of a policy-holder who confessed that, after a few drinks in the locker-room at the golf club, one of the members of his foursome announced that he sold insurance. Just to oblige the agent, all in the spirit of good fellowship, the man bought a large block of insurance. Yet he is rated a successful businessman, possessed of ability and shrewdness. We are almost at a loss to explain why such men, of more than average intelligence, are such greenhorns in their insurance dealings. Did you buy *your* insurance that way?

Insurance is the most vital part of your estate. When a legal matter comes up, you unhesitatingly seek the advice of your attorney. Even when the amount of money involved is small, you want to make sure you are represented, and right, before you go ahead. But in your insurance problems, no matter how much money is at stake, no matter if the fate of your wife and children hangs in the balance, you lay yourself wide open to the greed of a bungler.

But why labor the point?—they are insurance peddlers, dependent upon commissions for their livelihood. Their interest in you begins and ends in the amount of commission they will make out of the premiums you pay.

Your present insurance is what it is for the following reason:

Type of Policy	Amount of Protection	Premium (At Age 35)	Agent's Cut (Commission)
Ordinary Life (Participating).	$10,000	$ 281.10	$140.55
20-Payment Life ″ .	10,000	383.40	191.70
20-Year Endowment ″ .	10,000	519.10	155.73
10-Year Endowment ″ . *and*	10,000	1,058.70 *or*	211.74 *or*
1-Year Renewable Term (Non-Participating)	10,000	88.20	26.46

CHAPTER THIRTEEN

HOW TO ANALYZE A LIFE INSURANCE POLICY

Until you know how to analyze your policies, you are at a great disadvantage in all your insurance dealings. You are helpless before the persuasive arguments advanced by company and agent. Insurance, as we may have remarked before, is sold in such a distorted manner that the buyer never knows what he is getting. Indeed, he does not know how much his policies are costing him even after he has had them many years.

By showing you how to audit any policy correctly, we will remove your disadvantage. You will be able to calculate what your present insurance estate costs. By comparing that cost with the cost for Renewable Term policies, you will see exactly how much you would save by buying low-cost insurance and dropping your present high-priced contracts.

Audit

Mr. Jones is now 35 years old. At age 25, he

took out a $12,000 Convertible Twenty-Payment Life policy with a Mutual company. An examination of this policy reveals the following:

Face Amount of Policy............		$12,000.00
Loans on Policy..................	$1,500.00	
Cash in Policy (in Excess of Loans).	828.00	
Total Co-Insurance (Decreasing Company's Risk)		2,328.00
Net Risk to Company or Net Insurance (by Subtraction).........		$ 9,672.00

* * *

Premium-Payments	$372.24	
Dividend	48.12	
Current Year's Net Cost (Premium Minus Dividend)		$ 324.12
Interest Paid on $1,500 Loan at 6%.	90.00	
Interest Contributed on $828 Cash in Policy at 6%*................	49.68	
Total Interest Lost to Insured's Estate		139.68
Actual Cost for Net Insurance-Protection (Interest-Loss Plus Net Cost)		$ 463.80

* * *

Rate-Per-$1,000 of Insurance for Current Year (by Dividing Net Insurance Into Its Cost)........	$47.95	

* Money is worth six percent to Mr. Jones, since he can realize this percent by paying off a bank loan. When you audit your own policy, use whatever percent your cash can earn.

* * *

Having ascertained this excessive cost for his insurance, Mr. Jones saw at once that he could make a large saving by a substitution of policies. He purchased a new $12,000 One-Year Renewable Term policy. *After* the new contract was safely in his possession, he dropped the old contract. In other words, he did his own rewriting. Like all policy-holders he has been told many times that he "can change his insurance only at a loss to himself." Let us see how much Mr. Jones "loses":

The cost for One-Year Renewable Term (at age 35, the attained age of the insured) is $8.82 per thousand.

The cost for the full amount of the Renewable Term insurance ($12,000) is $105.84.

By cancelling the old policy, Mr. Jones retrieves $828, the amount of cash value in the policy. Moreover, he automatically rids himself of the loan of $1,500. On the retrieved cash, he starts earning interest; on the loan, he stops paying interest.

His new estate is the face amount of his new policy plus his retrieved cash, or a total of $12,828. This new estate costs him $105.84.

The amount of his former estate was $10,500 (the reduction being due to the loan of $1,500).

Therefore, the substitution has *increased* his estate by $2,328 (the difference between the new estate and the former estate).

The actual cost for his former estate of $10,500 was $463.80.

The actual cost for his new estate of $12,828 is $105.84.

By the substitution, he increases his estate by $2,328.

By the substitution, the amount of money he saves in the current year is $357.96.

Thus, by analyzing his policy, and correcting it accordingly, Mr. Jones effected a saving of $357.96 the first year, and increased his estate by $2,328. Mr. Jones has brought his insurance-and-investment program under his own control. When a dependent dies or becomes self-supporting, Mr. Jones plans to reduce his insurance in accordance with his new need for protection. If he desires, he can set up a savings-fund consisting of his retrieved cash value and his first year's saving of $357.96. He can, if he wishes, also add next year's saving to the fund. Adding the difference (between his new cost and what his cost would have been under the old policy) every year to the fund, and letting the entire amount accumulate at interest, Mr. Jones can eliminate his need for insurance. As he accumulates $1,000 on the outside, he can drop $1,000 of insurance, thereby eliminating the cost for that much insurance. With this process, if he lives, he will accumulate a fund of $12,000, and will have no need for any insurance. By reversing the methods of the insurance companies, he will have created his own unshackled endowment. If he should die before he endows himself, his beneficiary will receive both the death claim and the outside savings so far accumulated.   There are all sorts of variations to this plan.   Mr. Jones, on the basis of his own judgment, can mould it to suit himself.*

On the following page, we have prepared a blank audit sheet.   It may help you to analyze your own policies.   You may discover that you can effect a similar reduction of your insurance-costs.

---

*If the plan outlined here is not clear to you, refer to the section "Renewable Term—And Estate Planning" in Chapter Five.

BLANK AUDIT SHEET*

Face Amount of Policy............   (

Loans on Policy................... (

Cash in Policy (in Excess of Loans).. (————

Add to Get Total Co-Insurance
    (Decreasing Company's Risk).....   (————

Subtract to Get Net Risk to Com-
    pany or Net Insurance...........   (

* * *

Premium Payment................. (

Dividend .... (————

Subtract to Get Current Year's Net
    Cost ....   (

Interest Paid on Loans at____%
    (Whatever Percent Company
    Charges) .... (

Interest Contributed on Cash in
    Policy at _____% (Whatever Your
    Money can Earn) .... (

Add to Get Total Interest Lost to
    Estate ....   (————

Actual Cost for Net Insurance (In-
    terest Loss Plus Net Cost)........   (

* * *

Divide Net Insurance Into Cost For
    Net Insurance to Get Rate-Per
    $1,000 of Insurance for Current
    Year .... (

---

*Figures to be placed immediately after parenthesis sign.

CHAPTER FOURTEEN

HOW TO REWRITE YOUR POLICIES

Now that you appreciate the extent of the over-charges and liabilities in your present policies, you are ready for action. You want to revise your insurance estate; you want to cancel all policy-loans; you want to retrieve all cash values still in your policies; you want the interest to work for you—and not for the company; and, most important of all, you want to buy the best insurance you can get.

For the best insurance is also the cheapest insurance. The face amount of protection in the inexpensive Renewable Term policies never decreases, no matter how long you keep them. You will never co-insure yourself; you are going to separate your saving-program from your protection-program. And not until the companies start keeping a double ledger, not until they recognize saving and protection as independent programs, will you attempt to save with them.

YOU HAVE THE RIGHT TO CHANGE

Even though the companies are up in arms

against rewriting, remember that, as far as you are concerned, their powder is wet. You have the contractual right to buy and cancel any insurance you please. The company will try to make substitution difficult, but *legally* they can do nothing to stop you. Their "anti-twisting" laws apply only to company representatives, never to you. By carefully following the directions for rewriting or twisting, outlined in this chapter, you will give them no pretext to refuse to issue new insurance.

Plan Your Estate

Do not purchase the new insurance like you bought the old. Insurance exists for a definite purpose—to leave a lump sum of money or an income to your family in the event of your death. It is bought only to protect those who have a real insurable interest in you; you buy insurance for your dependents—and for no one else. Never buy it with the intention of saving; the method is too costly. And instead of buying insurance-protection in indiscriminate amounts, determine the needs of your dependents, and buy accordingly. Also, in the future, when the needs of your dependents decrease, you may correspondingly decrease the amount of insurance you carry.

Medical Examination

Have your own doctor give you a thorough physical examination, including a urine analysis, before you apply for new insurance. To let the company doctor examine you first, is a needless gamble. For, any ailment he finds, no matter how trivial or easily remedied, may give the company cause to reject you. Once you are found to be "uninsurable," the information is broadcast to every other company. This will handicap you in all further insurance dealings, whether they concern buying new insurance or re-instating old insurance.

If your own physician does not pass you, certainly a company doctor will not. In such a case, you cannot buy new insurance—not, at least, at the regular rates. Renewable Term insurance, in fact, is not sold at all to sub-standard risks. Your doctor may even find that your health is so impaired that you cannot expect to live much longer. In many cases, policy-holders could accept the option of extended term insurance, and stop all further premium payments. Before you do so, make reasonably certain that the period of extension insures you for the rest of your life. In a case of this kind, it is advisable to confer not only with your doctor but with any independent insurance counselor. But once your doctor decides that your health is satisfactory, you are ready for the company doctor. Even then, answer only those questions the latter asks you; do not volunteer any information: it can do you no good, and it may work harm.

Do Some Shopping

Satisfied that you are physically fit, your next step is to find a company that sells *Renewable Term*. We warn against calling your old agent. If he senses a twist, he will do everything possible to prevent it. And if he notifies the companies, a rewrite is almost impossible. Remember, you can expect no aid from him. If you have difficulty in finding a suitable company, write to your State Insurance Commissioner.

Application

There is a question included in your application which reads: "Is the policy for which you are hereby applying intended to take the place of insurance carried with this or any other company? If yes, give particulars."

If you answer "yes," you lessen the chance of getting the new insurance. Most applicants found that if the answer is "No", they get the new insurance with no difficulty. Of course, after you have the new insurance, you have every right to drop the old. What your intention was then, may not be your intention now. You can change your mind freely: that is your privilege.

Large Amounts

Do not attempt to replace the full amount of your insurance at one time if it is over $25,000.

Do it rather in small lots. And you may find it advisable to utilize several companies.

Where large amounts are concerned, the company makes a strict commercial examination; and if they decide you are carrying more insurance than your income warrants, they will refuse to issue the new business. Today, the companies rarely issue insurance totaling more than ten times the applicant's yearly income.

If you now carry a very large amount, you have probably been "coded". This is a recent gesture on the part of the companies further to forestall twisting. If you carry a large amount, and if the purchase of new insurance would make your total insurance estate more than ten times your income, you may be refused on the ground of being "over-insured". These cases call for special handling. We advise you to employ the services of an independent insurance counsellor, capable of guiding you through the intricacies of such a replacement.

Avoid Interest Charges on Semi-Annual or Quarterly Payments

Premiums should be paid on an annual basis only. If you pay on a semi-annual or a quarterly basis, the company adds an interest charge to your premiums. Thus, for the same policy, two semi-annual or four quarter-annual premiums total appreciably more than one annual premium.

Should you desire for the sake of convenience to make two or four small payments a year instead of one large one, you can do so without paying any interest. Instead of purchasing one $10,000 policy, for example, buy four $2,500 policies. All should be payable on an annual basis, but the anniversary dates should be specified to suit yourself. You can, that is to say, buy a policy on May 1st, but have the anniversary fall on November 1st. Until November 1st, you pay a *pro rata* premium, enough to carry the policy from its issue to the time of its anniversary when the annual premium falls due. By arranging your policies in this manner, you would have annual premiums on small policies coming due at definite dates, spaced on the basis best suited to your needs.

PAY THE PREMIUM AT ONCE

As soon as you receive the policy you want, pay the premium immediately. It is not in force until it is paid for; once the first premium is paid, it is your property.

Having secured part of the new amount desired, have your agent inquire through the manager of the Branch Office whether they will consider placing an additional amount. Have it appear as if the inquiry comes directly from the agent. Do not sign an application for additional insurance as yet. In this way, you will avoid a rejection or postponement which might be held against you when attempting to purchase in another company.

Applications always ask if you have been refused insurance by another company for any reason. If the request for additional insurance comes from the agent (as a suggestion that he might be able to sell it to you) the company's refusal (if they do refuse) refers to the agent and not to you. In this indirect manner, you prevent complications.

If the company refuses the agent, you can always go to another company, and, with intelligent handling, manage finally to get what you want.

How to Cancel

Once that all the new insurance you want is in your possession, with the first premiums paid, you are ready to abandon your liabilities by cancelling your old insurance. We suggest this method:

Carry all policies to their yearly anniversary, regardless of whether you pay annually, semi-annually, or quarterly. If you are paying on any basis other than annual, it may be advisable to make further payments to bring the policy to its annual birthday; because at this time cash surrender values increase (sometimes more than your premium-payment), and further "dividends" are declared (if in a participating company), which you are entitled to without paying the following year's premium. It is a refund due you from previous overcharges.

Then, two weeks before the last day of the grace-period, write to the company, requesting the policy cancelled, for its full cash surrender value, plus any dividends due or accumulated. There is no reason why you should cancel before that time. Your contract calls for protection during the grace period. Take advantage of it.

FALLACIOUS ARGUMENTS AGAINST THE TWIST
"You Are Older Now"

The first thing an agent who opposes a twist will tell you is that it doesn't pay to replace insurance because you bought your present insurance when you were younger. At your attained age insurance costs so much more that you must lose by a substitution.

Why the argument is false:

The basic cost of insurance in any year is the mortality cost for that year plus the overhead expenses. This cost must be met in any policy, no matter how old it is. You cannot avoid the increased rate; the basic cost must be deducted from your payments. If you recall our analyses of the various cash value policies, you will remember the actual cost to you not only goes up, but goes up far more than is necessary. In your present policy, you are more than paying for the increased mortality cost of your attained age.

"No Cash Values—No Non-Forfeiture Privileges"

The agent may point out that the new policy will create no cash value, and hence will not include such advantages as "paid-up insurance," "extended term insurance," and the "policy-loan privilege."

Why the argument is meaningless:

(1) With the Renewable Term policy, you will be buying protection only. The agent fails to mention that the difference you save by purchasing pure insurance-protection is in your possession, and not within the policy where it creates liabilities. You can utilize this difference in any manner you wish; you can save it on the outside, or spend it. Your use of it will not be confined to the terms of the contract.

(2) You will increase your estate by the amount of cash value you retrieve by cancelling your old policy. In your possession, it cannot be retained by the company at your death. You will also automatically cancel all policy-loans, upon which you are paying interest, and which are decreasing your gross protection.

(3) The interest you can earn on the retrieved cash is yours, to use in any manner you wish. If you want to apply it to the premium-payments on the new policy, it will help meet your premium-costs, and may even take care of them entirely.

(4) The various "non-forfeiture privileges" are

undesirable and costly; their existence is an expression of the extent of your overpayments. Their presence in a policy is irrefutable evidence that the contract is undesirable. That Renewable Term has none is its best recommendation.

"Your New Policy is Contestable"

(1) Your new policy is contestable only on the ground that you supplied false information concerning the medical, financial, and moral requirements. You answered these correctly when you bought your original policy. It was not contested. There is no reason that your new policy will be contested.

(2) The policy is not contestable for any other reasons than those above. Thousands of claims have been paid when death occurred during the period of contestability. They will continue to be paid.

(3) When you state in your application that you are buying the new insurance not to replace existing insurance, that is what you mean. If you happen to change your mind, and drop the old insurance later, that is your inalienable privilege. *No policy has ever been, or can ever be, contested on that ground.* There is $15,000,000,000 worth of new insurance written every year, a large portion of which is replacement. None of it has ever been contested on this question. So, unless you in-

tend to commit suicide, give no further thought to the incontestability clause. And remember that the contestability period lasts for only one or two years, after which time the policy is incontestable for any reason except non-payment of premiums.

"Your New Insurance Won't Have Income Disability"

This section concerns only those whose present insurance has income-disability. If you have it, the agent may tell you that once you drop it, you cannot get any more.

Why this is not true:

(1) A number of life insurance companies are still selling it at a slightly increased rate.

(2) There are many Accident and Health companies that have designed a non-cancellable income-disability policy practically identical to what you have. And since all companies continue to sell the Waiver of Premium Disability, you can easily duplicate what you have, if you still want it. And by separating it from your insurance-protection you will not have to sacrifice it if you find it necessary to drop your insurance.

(3) In any case we do not recommend it. Remember that before you are considered "totally and permanently disabled," you are practically dead. Records prove that almost all those eligible to collect die in a short time. Of the 296,626

policies terminated in 1933 in the New York Life Insurance Co., only 39 were terminated by disability.*

(4) Practically all participating companies have drastically reduced "dividends" on policies carrying income-disability. The average reduction is about 50%. Hence it is disadvantageous to carry it combined with life insurance.

Other Arguments

There are many other supposed "arguments" against a twist, too silly or trivial to discuss at length. The story that the agent must be paid a new large first-year commission, that this comes out of your premium, etc., is such an "argument". What the company does with your premium is, unfortunately, out of your control. Whether they pay the agent the commission or steal it under the "No Credit—No Commission," ruling, does not alter the fact that your new insurance is cheaper.

It must be distinctly understood that the success of a twist doesn't depend upon the interest-rate you can get on the retrieved cash. Use any interest factor you care to, and the results will speak for themselves. The important point is that you do not forfeit any accumulation saved outside the policy.

---

*Eighty-ninth Annual Report, New York Life Ins. Co., Dec. 31, 1933.

SUMMARY OF THE TWIST

1. You have the right to replace insurance.

2. It is important that the companies do not realize it is a rewrite until the whole transaction is completed. You know by now that the companies lose in a twist what you gain.

3. Plan your estate according to the needs of your dependents. By purchasing an amount you can afford to carry, you will be able to fulfill your program for them.

4. Have your own doctor examine you first, to make sure that you are still insurable. If you are, then you are ready for any examination given by a company physician. Answer his questions as accurately as you can, but don't volunteer information.

5. Shop around for a company that sells Renewable Term or Term Expectancy. Do not be satisfied with anything else.

6. It is unwise to go to the agent who sold you your present policy. If he thinks you intend to twist, he may notify the company—an act which may prevent you from getting new insurance. Never permit the agent handling you to learn that you contemplate dropping your present insurance.

7. A question in the application asks if you intend the new insurance to replace existing insurance. If you answer "yes", you may nullify your chance of getting the new insurance. Use your own judgment when answering that question. Most people answer "No." Later on, when the

new policy is in their possession with the first premium paid, they may change their minds and decide to drop the old insurance. There is nothing the company can do about it.

8. If you carry more than $50,000 worth of insurance, it is wiser not to try to do your own twisting. Get in touch with an independent insurance expert.

9. When you receive the Renewable Term policy you want, pay the premium at once. The policy is then yours and cannot be recalled by the company.

10. If the new policy is not the total amount of new insurance you want, have the agent ask the manager of his Branch Office if you can have more insurance. In all probability, you can. But if you cannot, you have not been rejected. Hence, you can apply to another company with an unblemished record.

11. Carry all old policies you intend to drop, to their yearly anniversary. Write to the company, two weeks before the last day of the grace period, requesting the policy cancelled for its cash surrender value, plus any dividends due or accumulated.

12. You will hear many silly arguments against the twist. None of them stand up under examination. In this book, we have exposed most of them. If you have understood our development of. the principles of insurance, you are prepared to refute any of the others.

CHAPTER FIFTEEN

A WORD TO BANKERS, ATTORNEYS AND ACCOUNTANTS

Bankers, attorneys, accountants—for such men as these, a thorough knowledge of life insurance is of double importance. It is important because they, too, are policy-holders and could correct their own insurance programs advantageously; it is of greater import because, due to the nature of their positions, other men rely upon them for impartial advice and guidance.

Unlike the companies and their agents, it is not to their benefit to mislead their clients. Theirs is a position of trust. But they cannot adequately guard the best interests of their clients if they overlook the insurance question. How many accountants, making an audit of a client's estate, think of examining his life insurance and intelligently checking its assets and liabilities? A knowledge of life insurance on the part of the accountant would enable him in many cases to reveal factors of strength and weakness hitherto unknown to the client. The acountant would be in a position to uncover reservoirs of available cash and to disclose practical ways and means of reducing current expenditures.

How many lawyers, advising upon estate planning, wills, and similar matters, know that the client could increase the size of his estate immediately at no extra cost, in addition to releasing sums of money for various present purposes, by a well-conceived insurance replacement? We know many attorneys who, heavily in debt, struggling along with sharply reduced incomes, carry exorbitantly priced Endowment insurance. With their own estates tottering, the question arises as to how much their advice on estate problems is worth.

How many bankers know enough about life insurance to realize that the insurance companies are their most pressing competitors? Many bankers recommend Endowments and Limited Payment Life policies without any suspicion that these contracts are not so much insurance policies as undesirable savings repositories. When bankers recommend such policies they are simply inviting depositors to take their banking business elsewhere. The banker has a community responsibility as an adviser in all financial problems. Unless he is versed in life insurance principles, he cannot very well fulfill that responsibility. He has a further responsibility to his bank; by neglecting the possibilities for good and evil in life insurance, he serves his bank badly.

A few examples will illustrate the vital importance of insurance knowledge to bankers. Mr. Jones, a manufacturer, made a $10,000 loan from a bank five years ago. Financial reverses have been such that he has been unable to repay the loan. The bank, making the best of it, has renewed the loan again and again. Recently, it demanded additional collateral; Mr. Jones accordingly assigned his $40,000 life insurance policy to the bank so that, in the event of his death at least, the loan will be made good. The picture is this: the bank needs the money but apparently it cannot get it; the debtor wants to repay the loan but he has no cash, and must, therefore, continue to groan under the interest burden.

Suppose the banker in this picture knew a little about life insurance and analyzed Mr. Jones' policy. Discovering a cash value of, let us say, $15,000 in the policy, he would suggest to Mr. Jones that he buy $40,000 of new, inexpensive Renewable Term insurance, and surrender his old policy. The results, some of them beneficial to the bank, some to the insured, and some to both, would include the following:

(1) The $10,000 loan could be immediately repaid to the bank.

(2) The insured would have an additional $5,000 in cash.

(3) The interest burden would cease.

(4) The insured would have effected a considerable reduction in his annual expenditure for insurance.

(5) He would be in a position to resume a banking account on a proper scale.

(6) His financial condition, his credit rating, would be greatly strengthened.

We know of a banker who compelled an attorney to take out a $100,000 20-Payment Life policy to cover a bank loan. In this case, neither the banker nor the lawyer knew the first thing about insurance. Instead of an annual premium of about $900 on a Renewable Term policy, the attorney paid more than $3,000. To make the situation even more ridiculous, the policy was purchased on a quarter-annual basis, on which, as everyone should know, the company levies an interest-charge. This charge can easily be avoided by purchasing the protection in a number of policies, all on an annual basis, but with their anniversary dates spaced according to the needs of the policy-holder. When the policies are received, the premium will be paid on a *pro rata* basis until the annual date, after which only annual premiums will be paid. The avoidable interest-charge in this instance would alone have bought $20,000 of insurance! Obviously, the deal was undertaken at the behest of an ignorant or unscrupulous agent—the only one who profited by the transaction. Where the banker had a chance to help the attorney pay back the bank loan, he forced him to enter into a new, dubious investment scheme which could work only harm to both the bank and his client.

Enough has been said to show how much bankers, accountants and attorneys could gain from a realistic study of life insurance. It is patently inexcusable for them to neglect their clients' insurance programs. Many businessmen, hard-pressed for cash, go to extreme lengths to get credit and loans of all sorts, including policy-loans. Why are their insurance policies not analyzed with a view toward determining the extent of the unfettered cash they could retrieve? The accountant or attorney who is capable of steering his clients through the intricacies of the rewrite, wins the undying gratitude and loyalty of these clients. A carefully considered replacement of expensive insurance and its attendant liabilities by Renewable Term or Term Expectancy can often bolster up an unsound financial condition, besides rescuing the client's insurance program from eventual lapse.

Remember that your clients have no one to guide them in such matters except you. It is your duty to them to act as their insurance counsellor, to consider their insurance problems with the minutest care. We know for a certainty that several attorneys and accountants have saved many thousands of dollars for clients by utilizing the very methods we recommend.

CHAPTER SIXTEEN

POLICY-HOLDERS MUST ORGANIZE

Millions of policy-holders, bewildered by the persistent criminal indifference of the life insurance companies to their plight, are beginning to demand a showdown. The four-billion-dollar loan which they have made from their beneficiaries continues to exact an interest toll of a quarter-of-a-billion. With protection decreased by the amount of four billion dollars, a greater burden of costs prevails.

Insurance estates—mis-planned at the start, and never corrected—crumble. Behind the statistical computation of the enormous lapse-rate, lie the unrecorded, tragic case histories of unprotected dependents. With the companies offering no assistance and preventing their agents from giving any, with policy-holders themselves kept ignorant of what to do, the discontent of policy-holders everywhere is beginning to smoulder. The constant barrage of sugary advertising which the companies administer as a soothing syrup for policy-holders is placating few. Its studied irrelevance only adds to the grudge against the companies.

True, a few policy-holders have been aided by independent counselors, or by twisters. Others who read this book will find a partial solution. But for the remaining vast majority, nothing is being done.

Yet something must be done to allay this mass discontent. Left to itself, left to nourish on the grievances of a betrayed army of policy-holders, such discontent might have serious repercussions. In order to blunt its edge, in order to dissipate it harmlessly, a senatorial investigation into the abuses of life insurance is being planned. Senator Fletcher, Chairman of the Senate Banking Committee, has urged President Roosevelt to back a sweeping inquiry into the operation of life insurance companies. Such an investigation is bound to come. The policy-holder will see his company battered from pillar to post—in newspaper headlines. Are policy-holders in need of aid? They will get a three-ring circus, a sham battle staged in a Senate ante-room, to divert their attention from their real grievances.

Suppose the investigators do air the corruption of legislatures and public opinion, the exorbitant costs of writing insurance, the lavish salaries and bonuses bestowed upon company officials; suppose the testimony irrefutably demonstrates that policy-holders' funds have been badly invested, that sons and cousins and uncles of officials can almost automatically become officials also, that the House of

Morgan controls the largest companies and that the latter dominate the smaller companies through the device of interlocking directorates. Let us take a nose-dive into optimism, and even suppose that, following the investigation, Congress will enact legislation that will attempt to curb some of these abuses. What of it?

Can the slashing of salaries also slash your insurance-costs? Will the dismissal of a few brothers-in-law liquidate the liabilities in millions of policies? What, in other words, will the investigation intended to help policy-holders, really do to help them? Nothing.

Are we unduly pessimistic? We think not: past experience forces us into that unpleasant conclusion. There has been an investigation, similar to the one proposed, that sought to probe the misconduct of life insurance companies in New York State. The scandals brought to light by the Hughes-Armstrong Investigation (1905-06) compelled the State Legislature to consider certain reforms, intended presumably to correct the abuses. "The reforms suggested," according to the comment of *The Independent,* a prominent weekly of the time, "are designed chiefly to withdraw the business of life insurance, as it has been conducted by the greatest of American Companies, from the control of millionaire speculators and greedy executive officers, and to confine it within legitimate limits; to prohibit technical methods which have served the interests of unworthy managers rather than those of the policy-holder; to prevent the use of policy-holders' money for the corrupt purchase or prevention of legislation; and to give policy-holders that influence in the management of mutual companies which it is their right to exercise . . . recommendations of great importance, which, if carried into legislation, will be of enduring service to the public."*

It was a great progressive, if ingenuous, era. The recommendations were hailed by all right-minded people; editorials were written; sermons were delivered; it was the New Deal for policy-holders. As *Harpers Weekly* said, "The most satisfying feature of the report of the Armstrong committee . . . is the cheering indication that our legislative bodies are still capable of doing a thorough job." Duly impressed, the New York State legislative body passed reform measures.

Ten years later, a different Mr. Armstrong wrote a book called *License to Steal,* dealing with the insurance companies, the Investigation, and the corrective laws. We quote Mr. Armstrong:

> "The worst and most corrupt insurance laws ever enacted in any country or state were the 'reform' laws following the Hughes Investigation of 1905, and introduced as the recommendations

---

*The Independent, March 1, 1906.

of the committee. They seemed fair on their face; the slaving agents were struck hard; certain immoral policies were suppressed; but certain innocent-looking phrases not found in any dictionary—phrases that no one can understand and that have never been defined, piled up bigger reserves and authorized bigger expenses . . ."

Reformers are many; reforms few. Let us be realistic. What concrete benefits—for the consumer, not the producer—have resulted from other investigations in the past? To expect the government to resolve the undying contradiction between consumer and producer at the expense of the producer, is to succumb to a naive idealism. Upon the alter of profits, not only the interests of the consumers, but human life itself, is sacrificed. The Munitions Investigation is still fresh in your memory.

A little of what the Senate Munitions Committee uncovered was concisely put by a writer in *The Nation* (October 3, 1934):

> "The committee has demonstrated that the armament industry has fomented war scares, sold instruments of death to both sides in civil wars and international wars, bribed government officials at home and abroad, blocked armament embargoes, disregarded treaties of peace, interfered with disarmament conferences, lobbied for armament programs, employed spies in foreign armies, used army and navy officers as sales-promotion agents, profiteered at the expense of govern-

ments, participated in secret international agree-
ments for splitting profits and dividing world
markets, and sold patents and secret designs to
foreign countries. Each of these charges has
been established by correspondence taken from
the files of the American armament corporations
and amplified by the sworn statements of armament officials."

Will anything be done about it? At the present
time, the results of the Investigation are buried
beneath such slogans as "Take the profits out of
war," "Conscript capital as well as labor." The
consequence of the latter may be a regimentation
of labor during the next war—with the corollary,
the reduction of wage standards. But those who
traffic in the tools of destruction and death will not
be molested. For as soon as it became apparent
that the Nye committee was about to make significant disclosures, three rival committees were
launched to confuse public opinion and to white-
wash the munitions makers. Their "indefensible
business" (Senator Borah's phrase) is in little
danger of governmental interference.

* * *

In 1933, when the Democratic Party rode into
power on a tidal wave of social discontent, its plat-
form was dedicated to reform. One of the first
important moves of the new administration was
the drafting of food and drug legislation to drive

out quacks, adulterators, and poisoners. The public applauded. Here, at last, it was generally believed, profits of anti-social manufacturers were to be sacrificed for the protection of the consumer.

"Consumers' Research, Inc.," an organization that advises consumers in their daily purchases, describes what happened: "Here was an administration bill . . . a legislative measure designed to protect the sick, the ignorant, and the poverty-stricken from the greed of the most disreputable —and recognizably disreputable—group in the capitalist order. What happened? The bill was turned over to this group to sponsor, revise, and steer through Congress. . . ."

Arthur Kallet, an official of Consumers' Research and co-author of *100,000,000 Guinea Pigs*, comments in an article in the *New Masses:*

> "Imagine the Senate's going to dope peddlers for advice on how to curb the illegal sale of narcotics; to practising kidnapers to ask what punishment kidnapers deserve; to thugs for their ideas on how to protect the public welfare! Yet the witnesses who gravely advised the Senate—through the sympathetic medium of Dr. Copeland—on the curbing of food, drug, and cosmetic racketeers, represented the racketeers themselves. These good businessmen, whose ideas will be written into the Federal statute books if a new law is passed, have been responsible for greater robbery of the poor, for more suffering and more deaths than all the criminal inmates of all the

jails of the country. But because they prey only upon consumers, not upon other businessmen; and because they help support and control the press with hundreds of millions of dollars of advertising, they are respectable, and Congress will do their bidding."

The object-lesson of all this is rather simple. When the interests of the consumers conflict with the profits of the producers, all that the powerful vested interests must do is to pull the strings that manipulate the puppets in public office. By now it is common knowledge that the "medicine men" (gallantly assisted by newspapers and magazines full of patent medicine advertisements) wrote the legislation that was originally intended to protect the consumer. The defendant became his own Judge, Jury, Prosecution and—he needed no Defense. The consumer never had a chance. As Consumers' Research pointed out, "A year and a half has passed; the poisoning still goes on."

Do you suppose that the insurance companies, part of the empire controlled by the ubiquitous House of Morgan, have a less powerful lobby in Washington than the patent-medicine boys? If legislation is ever written to regulate the insurance companies, the companies themselves will write it. And history will repeat itself with a new "Armstrong" writing a new *License to Steal*," attacking the "Insurance-Reform Laws" of 19—.

Policy-holders cannot afford to wait for the gov-

ernment to help them.   It is dangerous, in fact, to
have any illusions about the efficacy of such help.
But there is no need to wait.

WHAT CAN BE DONE

Individually, your best weapon is the twist.
You do not have to rely on legislation. You can
start at once to correct some of the abuses in your
policies. You know the exact method to be followed; you have been forewarned of all the
stratagems the companies have (to date) at their
disposal. If policy-holders were to buy Renewable
Term insurance, salvage cash, cancel loans, and to
separate forever their savings from their protection, laws to restrain the companies would be almost unnecessary. Most of the extravagances of
the companies would be immediately stopped. It
is only because they have so much of your money
to squander that many of their excesses are
possible.

But policy-holders have another weapon. Like
any other group with common interests, they could
make great gains by organizing. When the chain
stores began making inroads into the business of
the small independent merchants, the latter faced
economic annihilation. If they had waited for
legislation to protect them, they would long since
have gone under. But by organizing into associa-
tions, by presenting a united front against their

common menace, their collective strength was effective. So, too, policy-holders must organize.

It is unfortunate that Consumers' Research, Inc. —"a strictly non-profit . . . organization which studies and reports on goods and services from the point of view of their selection, purchase, and use by the ultimate consumer"—neglects the important field of life insurance. Such an organization, employing unbiased actuaries and independent insurance counsellors, could serve the insurance-buyer as it now serves the commodity-buyer.

If policy-holders are to get aid from the companies, it is by now quite clear that they cannot accomplish a great deal singly. An organized group, expressing the collective will and needs of its membership, could force long overdue adjustments from the companies. Where the companies would ignore the individual, they would listen respectfully to a large group. Where the individual policy-holder can only request, an organization could demand.

Moreover, since the lion's share of the insurance business is handled by mutual companies, it is not impossible that changes of enduring benefit to policy-holders could be achieved through company elections. Although the fact is well-nigh ignored, it should be remembered that the sole owners of these mutual companies are their policy-holders, whose votes—theoretically—determine the management. At present, only a few thousand votes are cast in the elections—out of a possible electorate of millions. An organization, by voting its membership *en bloc* by proxy, could play an important role in these elections, and see to it that the company is run on a truly mutual basis, for the benefit of policy-holders.

The genuine service that such an organization could give its members by supplying them with information and help on their day to day insurance problems, cannot be over-emphasized. We have advised our readers, on several specific questions, to seek counsel from independent insurance experts. It is regrettable that few such experts exist; we recognize that you might run into difficulty in locating one. An organization of policy-holders could employ a few experts to serve the needs of the entire membership. Such problems as planning one's estate, when and how to accept specific options in the various policies, how to negotiate the difficulties of rewriting, the choice of a suitable company, in short, any problem which requires expert attention, could be handled best by an organization created by and for policy-holders. Such a group, of necessity, must have no commercial connections, direct or indirect, with any insurance company. It would have nothing to do with selling insurance. It would be purely advisory and representative.

In summary, then, you cannot depend on governmental aid, the companies are unwilling to help you, agents are prevented from giving you honest service, there is an insufficient number of independent insurance experts, and—life insurance itself being what it is—your only effective weapon, next to rewriting, is to organize.

THE END